EVIL

and the

PROCESS GOD

Barry L. Whitney

Toronto Studies in Theology
Volume 19

The Edwin Mellen Press
New York and Toronto

Library of Congress Cataloging in Publication Data

Whitney, Barry L.
  Evil and the process God.

  Bibliography: p.
  Includes indexes.
  1. Theodicy--History of doctrines--20th century.
2. God--History of doctrines--20th century. 3. Process
theology. 4. Hartshorne, Charles, 1897--   .
I. Title.
BT160.W524 1985   231'.8   84-25505
ISBN 0-88946-760-9

Toronto Studies in Theology
Series ISBN 0-88946-975-X

Printed in the United States of America

DEDICATION

To my wife, Mary,
and our children,
Christopher,
Matthew,
and Lara

CONTENTS

ACKNOWLEDGEMENTS

Grateful acknowledgement is made for use of specified excerpts from the following sources:

Man's Vision of God and the Logic of Theism, by Charles Hartshorne. Copyright 1941, renewed 1968, by Charles Hartshorne. Reprinted by permission of Harper and Row, Publishers, Inc.

The Divine Relativity: A Social Conception of God, by Charles Hartshorne. Copyright 1948. Reprinted by permission of Yale University Press.

A Natural Theology for Our Time, by Charles Hartshorne. Copyright 1967. Reprinted by permission of The Open Court Publishing Company, La Salle, Illinois.

The Logic of Perfection and Other Essays in Neoclassical Metaphysics, by Charles Hartshorne. Copyright 1962. Reprinted by permission of The Open Court Publishing Company, La Salle, Illinois.

Creative Synthesis and Philosophic Method, by Charles Hartshorne. Copyright 1970. Reprinted by permission of The Open Court Publishing Company, La Salle, Illinois.

"A New Look at the Problem of Evil," by Charles Hartshorne, in F. C. Dommeyer, ed., Current Philosophical Issues: Essays in Honor of Curt John Ducasse. Copyright 1966. Reprinted by permission of Charles C. Thomas, Publisher, Springfield, Illinois.

"Can There Be Proofs for the Existence of God?," by Charles Hartshorne, in R. H. Ayers and W. T. Blackstone, eds., Religious Language and Knowledge. Copyright 1972. Reprinted by permission of The University of Georgia Press.

PREFACE

The problem of evil (technically referred to as "theodicy") remains one of the most perplexing challenges to belief in the God of Christianity. Yet, at the same time, the important contributions which process philosophers and theologians have made toward a clarification and possible resolution of this problem have been largely ignored. Book after book on the problem of evil is published with virtually no consideration of the process thought developed by Alfred North Whitehead, Charles Hartshorne, and their intellectual descendants. The most notable exception is the 1968 study, Evil and the Concept of God, by Peter Hare and Edward Madden. Michael Galligan, in God and Evil (1976), also devotes some attention to the process thinkers' understanding of theodicy, and it is encouraging to see that John Hick has made up, somewhat, for ignoring process thought in his monumental Evil and the God of Love (1966) by including a brief discussion of it in the third edition of his Philosophy of Religion (1983). Within the ranks of process thinkers, there has been an almost equal lack of critical attention to the theodicy issue. Despite several unpublished dissertations and a handful of articles, David Griffin has published the only full-length study of the issue from the perspective of process thought in his informed and scholarly <u>God, Power, and Evil: A Process Theodicy</u> (1976), a book which unfortunately is now out of print. The voluminous writings of Whitehead and Hartshorne, of course, contain numerous references to the theodicy issue, but they do not present their arguments systematically.

The purpose of this present study is to reconstruct and critically assess the <u>process theodicy</u> that has been developed by Charles Hartshorne. I shall argue that Hartshorne has in fact two approaches to the theodicy issue. One is based on his theistic proofs and the subsequent contention that since God's existence is a necessary truth, no physical realities-- of which evil is the most obviously pressing instance--can count decisively against his existence. Hartshorne's second approach, however, seeks to show that God's power and benevolence can in fact be reconciled with the physical reality of evil and suffering in the world. This latter theodicy is, I believe, the more promising and potentially influential of the two, and the greater portion of the book will be devoted to a critical discussion of it. A number of its main themes will be considered: the revised conception of God in process thought; the understanding of creatures as partially autonomous centers of creativity; the free will solution; the all-important aesthetic considerations; the question of immortality; and the teaching that evil is overcome by God.

Central to process theodicy is an understanding of God which process thinkers believe is at odds with (what they refer to as) <u>traditional</u> or <u>classical theism</u>--a label they apply to the great majority of theologians throughout Christian history. Process thinkers criticize the traditional Christian doctrine of God as thoroughly inadequate and in need of drastic revision. In place of the all-determining, immutable, independent and unaffected God of traditional Christianity, process thinkers have developed a theism which, they insist, is far more religiously adequate and philosophically viable. I must point out, however, that much of the process thinkers' critique of traditional Christian theism is a hotly disputed point. In my opinion the critique is valid, yet I do not propose to attempt to justify this opinion with a detailed critical assessment of traditional theism. David Griffin has admirably accomplished this task in his aforementioned God, Power, and Evil and I would direct the reader to this study and to the writings of other process thinkers, especially those of Charles Hartshorne (see in particular his book, Philosophers Speak of God).

My present concern is to systematically present the process theodicy developed largely by Hartshorne, to contrast his theodicy with the traditional Christian theodicies, and to address a number of critical questions which arise, questions which have to do not only with external critiques but also with matters of internal consistency and coherence. It is my hope that this study will contribute, however modestly, to a furthering of scholarly interest in the contributions of process thought to the theodicy issue. The book is addressed to all those who share an interest in the seeking of new understanding and insight into what is clearly one of the most problematic issues faced by religious thinkers. A specialist's knowledge of process thought is not a prerequisite and, in fact, for the sake of a more general readership, I have included many passages which will provide the non-specialist with at least a preliminary indication of how process thought conceives various general themes which are relevant to the theodicy issue.

Portions of the book have appeared elsewhere, in somewhat altered versions. Part Two utilizes my "Divine Immutability in Process Philosophy and Contemporary Thomism," Horizons, Journal of the College Theology Society (1980), 49-68; "Rahner and Hartshorne on Divine Immutability," co-authored with J. Norman King, International Philosophical Quarterly (1982), 195-209; "Process Theism: Does a Persuasive God Coerce?," The Southern Journal of Philosophy (1979), 133-143; "Does God Influence the World's Creativity?: Hartshorne's Doctrine of Possibility," Philosophy Research Archives (1981), 613-622; and "Charles Hartshorne," in J. T. Culliton, ed., Non-violence--Central to Christian Spirituality (New York and Toronto: The Edwin Mellen Press, 1982), 217-237. Part Three utilizes my "Hartshorne's New Look at Theodicy," Studies in Religion (1979), 281-291.

This book is the product of many years of reflection on the theodicy issue, during which time I have incurred many debts. I am particularly grateful to my colleagues and students for the intellectual stimulation they provide and to Dr. John C. Robertson, Jr. who competently nurtured my interest in philosophical theology and exposed its great rewards. The influence of the writings of Alfred North Whitehead and, even more so, Charles Hartshorne on my intellectual development has been immense and I would not even like to imagine what the quality of my life would have been like without their great wisdom. To Dr. Hartshorne, moreover, I am indebted for his personal kindness and generous availability. I have also learned much from the writings of David Griffin and Lewis Ford. I am grateful to my colleague, Dr. Roy C. Amore, for his friendly critique and encouragement in the writing of this book. I wish to express my gratitude also to the competent operators in the Word Processing Centre here at the University of Windsor, and to Miss Shirley Fields for so quickly and accurately typing the text. And finally, I must acknowledge the patient understanding of my wife, Mary, who has endured my devotion to long hours of academic pursuits. This book is dedicated to her, and to our children: Christopher, Matthew, and Lara.

                        Barry L. Whitney
                        Windsor, Ontario, Canada

PART ONE: THE PROBLEM OF EVIL

Christian theologians have labored for centuries to explain why the world contains so much evil and suffering. More specifically, the problem has been to explain why belief in the Christian God, defined as an all-powerful and all-loving perfection, is not inconsistent with the reality of evil in the world. This book discusses the problem of evil from the perspective of the process thought derived mainly from the philosophical writings of Alfred North Whitehead (1861-1947) and, more directly, Charles Hartshorne (1897--). Process thought is a significant movement in contemporary philosophy and theology, and yet, as noted in the Preface, its contributions to the theodicy issue have not been adequately explored.[1] This perhaps is due to the philosophical complexity of process metaphysics and even more so to the somewhat severe and disconcerting critiques of the more traditional theology launched by process thinkers. It may be due, furthermore, to the fact that neither Whitehead nor Hartshorne has presented the process theodicy in a systematic fashion. Yet, fortunately, the application of process thought to the theodicy issue is a fairly straightforward one, and its contribution to the present discussion is far too substantial and significant to be ignored much longer. My own bias is a general enthusiasm and support for Hartshorne's contributions to the theodicy issue, although there are some points which are in need of clarification

and others which, as I shall argue, are in need of some
modification. The end result, nevertheless, is a strong
and viable theodicy which, while not fully conclusive (for
it is, afterall, a human enterprise), goes some distance
toward illuminating and resolving this issue which has
plagued us for centuries.

Chapter 1: GOOD AND EVIL

It is clearly evident that our world contains not only much joy and goodness but also vast amounts of evil and suffering. There is, on the one hand, much in life to celebrate, much which can instill in us an optimistic, positive sense of peace and well-being. We are fortunate indeed if we have experienced the serene beauty of a dampened forest or the majestic expanse of open sea; or again, if we have been deeply moved and comforted by the awesome and mysterious vault of the starry heavens on a quiet evening, or shared the joys of intimate fellowship, or the indescribable love of a parent for his children. Such moments are to be cherished, for they somehow assure the longing soul of its communion with a Presence which animates all life by its love and care. Mystical writings burst with references to these experiences and they may encourage and comfort all of us in our darker moments. The following testimony is both typical and stunning:

> I was alone upon the seashore as all these thoughts flowed over me, liberating and reconciling; and now again, as once before in distant days in the Alps of Dauphiné, I was impelled to kneel down, this time before the illimitable ocean, symbol of the Infinite. I felt that I prayed as I had never prayed before, and knew now what prayer really is: to return from the solitude of individuation into the

consciousness of unity with all that is, to kneel
down as one that passes away, and to rise up as
one   imperishable.   Earth,   heaven,   and   sea
resounded   as   in   one   vast   world-encircling
harmony.   It   was   as   if   the   chorus   of   all   the
great who had ever lived were about me.   I felt
myself one with them.[2]

Such   experiences   may   be   more   profoundly   mystical
than the fleeting and superficial glimpses of those of us
who are unable, for whatever reasons, to intuit as deeply
the spiritual dimension of life, yet it is difficult to
imagine any human life which has not had some moments of
mystical or "religious experience" -- at least as a vague
and   unsustained   approximation   of   the   full   mystical
vision.[3]   Non-theists   may   not   be   willing   to   associate
such   intuitions   with   a   divine   referent,   but   from   the
Christian perspective these experiences are nothing less
than   intuitions   of   God,   encounters   with   the   divine
presence.[4]   Rudolph Otto, in The Idea of the Holy, has
given a classic account of the spiritual reality intuited
in religious experience: it is the "numinous," the "wholly
other," which fills the mystic with awe and dread, and
which comforts with a deep, unutterable peace.[5]   Those of
us who are not mystics rely upon the testimony of mystics
and prophets to disclose the profound religious truths they
have experienced.   We give assent to their insights when we
realize that they make more explicit what we have already
felt implicitly or vaguely in our own deeper moments.[6]
The   language   and   rituals   of   the   world's   religions
conceptualize and act out these insights, and thereby help
us to come to terms with them, to appropriate them and
harvest their benefits.

There is, unfortunately, a darker side to our lives
with which we must also come to terms. Millions of living
souls suffer in mental and physical anguish. Countless
children die in squalor and malnutrition; nature's forces
arbitrarily wreck havoc, and the infamous inhumanity human
beings display toward one another, to say nothing about our
wanton and disgraceful callousness with regard to lesser
life forms and to the environment, lead to incalculable
destruction and misery. The eighteenth century
philosopher, David Hume, has documented in all-too-tragic
vividness, the ills to which the world's creatures are heir:

> The whole earth ... is cursed and polluted. A
> perpetual war is kindled amongst all living
> creatures. Necessity, hunger, want stimulate the
> strong and courageous; fear, anxiety, terror
> agitate the weak and infirm. The first entrance
> into life gives anguish to the newborn infant and
> to its wretched parent; weakness, impotence,
> distress attend each stage of that life, and it
> is, at last, finished in agony and horror.
> Observe too ... the curious artifices of nature
> in order to embitter the life of every living
> being. The stronger prey upon the weaker and
> keep them in perpetual terror and anxiety. The
> weaker, too, in their turn, often prey upon the
> stronger, and vex and molest them without
> relaxation .... every animal is surrounded with
> enemies which incessantly seek his misery and
> destruction.[7]

Hume notes, in disgust, the particularly human evils, the
"[o]ppression, injustice, contempt, contumely, violence,
sedition, war, calumny, treachery, [and] fraud" by which we

"mutually torment each other."[8]   It seems true, as Jesuit
scholar G. H. Joyce has noted, that if we focus our
attention upon the miseries of life, be they of human or
natural origin, "we may be led to wonder how God came to
deal so harshly with His Creatures as to provide them with
such a home,"[9] and with such devastating capabilities.

THE PROBLEM OF EVIL

        In face of this darker side of life, a discomforting
melancholy may overtake the soul and inundate it with a
sense of hopeless despair and meaninglessness. The joys of
life, in such moments, may be all but overshadowed, and we
come face to face with the agonizing problem which has
gnawed at our hearts for centuries: the so-called problem
of evil. How can we believe that life is ultimately
meaningful and guided by the providential care of an
omnipotent and omnibenevolent God when all around us there
is so much evil and misery? If God really is all-powerful,
why does he not more actively control the lives of his
creatures and permit less evil? If God is all-loving, if
he really is the morally perfect Being conceived by
Christian theology, why has he not used his power to create
(or permit) only that which is just and good for his
creatures? Since, however, evil and suffering are very
much a part of our world, are we not forced to conclude
that either God is not willing to prevent evil, or that he
is not able to do so, or both? And if this is the case,
can we continue to believe in the providential care of an
omnipotent and omnibenevolent being, a being "that than
which nothing greater can be conceived" ("aliquo quid maius
cogitari est," Anselm)?[10] Perhaps, as sceptics conclude,
the Christian God simply does not exist! The burden, it
seems to me, is on the shoulders of Christian theologians

to explain why an omnipotent and omnibenevolent deity would permit (or perhaps himself even cause) so much evil and suffering. It is, as the contemporary theologian John Hick points out, not the sceptic but the theologian who is obliged to explain the universe, for it is the latter "who claims that the situation is other than it appears, that there is an invisible divine Being who is perfect in goodness and unlimited in power. And the problem of evil arises at this point as a genuine difficulty that he is bound to face. _Si deus est_, _unda malum?_"[11]

There is, unfortunately, no simple solution to this problem, and despite persistent reflection and debate among the greatest theological minds over the past two millennia, the problem of evil remains a major and devastating threat to Christian hope and faith. Few contemporary religious thinkers are willing to claim that past attempts to solve this perplexing problem are fully convincing, and indeed anyone who reflects seriously on the problem must contend with an impressive array of sceptical arguments _against_ the traditional Christian solutions. In the meantime, we are still confronted not only with the _intellectual_ or _theoretical_ problem of evil--that is, explaining its source and meaning, and reconciling it with belief in God--but also with the acute _existential_ or _practical_ problem, that of coping with evil, reducing and overcoming it, and maintaining an intimate and personal _faith_ in God despite the intermittent ravagings of our lives by tragedy and pain.

Many would argue that the theoretical problem is unsolvable because the ultimate explanation for evil lies beyond our comprehension. They focus their attention, accordingly, solely upon practical methods to cope with evil, engaging, for example, in a wide variety of

humanitarian services (social agencies and the like).[12]
This approach, however, hardly seems sufficient, for our
intellectual nature demands that we confront the
theoretical issue directly. Otherwise, the faith and trust
we have in God, which helps us cope with evil, may be less
than adequate to sustain us. Thinking Christians seek and
need explanations for evil and an understanding of its
relationship to God. And traditional Christian theology
has, of course, supplied an abundance of such
explanations. But before turning to a critical discussion
of them, I wish first to consider the "faith solution."

Chapter 2: THE FAITH SOLUTION

The faith solution often takes the form of encouraging the belief that all earthly events, all goods and evils, are the direct result of the omnibenevolent will and omnipotent causal agency of God. It cautions, furthermore, that human beings have no right to question the divine distribution of goods and evils, since God's plan for his creation is clearly beyond the reach of human comprehension. It encourages the belief, in short, that everything which happens has a "morally sufficient reason,"[13] that (as the poet Alexander Pope put it) "whatever is, is right."[14] One finds a classic presentation of this solution in the Book of Job, and it has persisted unabated throughout the centuries to the present day. Common funeral parlor talk, for example, usually includes the consoling comment that the deceased died because of God's will, that the loved one's death serves some meaningful purpose in God's incomprehensible plan.[15]

The faith solution, moreover, commonly encourages the focusing of one's faith and trust in the Bible. It encourages the acceptance of a number of biblical explanations for the origin and meaning of the world's evils: evil is seen as a divine punishment for human sins, or as a divine warning; it is seen as a test of faith; or attributed to satanic powers; or to human free will; and so on--these themes will be discussed later in this chapter and in the following chapter.

NEGATIVE IMPLICATIONS

There can be no question as to the privileged position the faith solution has held in Christian thought over the centuries. It has an undeniable appeal and positive value, providing not only an amazingly simple solution to the problem of evil, but also giving comfort and hope to lives which otherwise might succumb to despair in face of the pain and anguish they are called upon to endure. But there are also negative implications, indeed serious negative implications, which greatly reduce its effectiveness and viability.[16] It can, for example, easily contribute to a mesmerizing fatalism which rationalizes away any human responsibility for evil. For while it may be comforting and reassuring to find meaning and significance in daily events by attributing all goods and evils to the direct causal agency of God, such an attitude often produces a destructive resignation, a numbing despair that we have no control over our lives. It can induce feelings which lead to irresponsible and unjustifiable social inactivity, to an abdication of our social responsibilities (as we rationalize the existence of personal and social evils as God's will and plan). The poor and the wretched will indeed be with us always, as long as we are content to believe that all things are in the hands of God. One can only empathize with third world theologians like Brazilian Archibishop Dom Helder Camara in their hard-fought efforts to overcome this destructive fatalism and misguided faith.[17]

The faith stance, moreover, not only can inculcate this deplorable attitude, but it is simply, and just as

problematically, an unrealistic option for many people. We
cannot, quite frankly, exhort others to "have faith" in
God's providential care despite the evil and anguish which
devastate their lives, for it is often this very evil which
retards their potential openness to faith and hope! And
this is all the more true for those reflective Christians
who feel a sincere obligation to strengthen their
spirituality by seeking a deeper understanding--rather than
a mere blind acceptance--of their religious beliefs. Such
people take seriously Jesus' commandment that we love God
not only with our hearts and souls, but also with our
minds. Serious and dedicated intellectual reflection about
the content of our religious beliefs is anything but
impious, despite those who would so condemn it. Informed
study and reflection is for many people an essential task
which strengthens and significantly deepens their faith;
indeed, it is indispensable if their faith is to remain an
active part of their lives.[18]

THE "FALL" OF ADAM AND EVE

There are many Christians, nevertheless, who
continue to focus their faith and trust on the Bible,
accepted more or less literally, and without much critical,
intellectual reflection, as the basic explanation for the
world's evils. In particular, the Genesis account of Adam
and Eve is perceived as accounting for the origin of evil
in a world which otherwise would have remained a utopic
garden. The biblical account attributes evil to the "fall"
of the first human pair into sin and, consequently, to the
misguided choices of their tainted progeny, and also to the
just punishment of God for these transgressions. This
explanation was to become the dominant teaching about evil

in the Old Testament world. It was utilized in the greatly
influential writings of St. Paul, furthermore, and has had
a central and privileged place in "virtually all subsequent
Christian thought concerning sin and evil."[19] The past
two centuries of biblical scholarship, however, and modern
scientific findings over an even longer period, have made
it less than prudent to interpret this biblical story (and
many others) as though it were a record of actual
historical fact. It represents, rather, religious insight,
conceptualized in the language and thought-forms of the
ancient biblical world view. We now realize that the
Genesis account of the "fall" is but one of the world's
great myths which seeks to explain the source and meaning
of evil and to comprehend its relationship to God.[20] The
term "myth," of course, has a very different meaning in
theology than in secular thought. While the latter
defines myth as a falsehood or untruth, in theology myth is
understood as a non-literal conceptualization of religious
truth. Myths put religious insights into words (in story
form), and while the truths expressed by the myths are not
scientifically (empirically) verifiable, they are,
nevertheless, regarded by those who accept and partake in
the myths as viable insights into the nature of reality.[21]

Contemporary Christians need not feel any absolute
religious or moral obligation to interpret literally the
biblical myth of the "fall." Indeed, it is both tragic and
misguided to believe that one's religiosity, one's
Christianity, is supposedly measured by one's willingness
to accept the Bible literally or not at all. Yet it is
such an all-or-nothing attitude which the conservative and
literalist Christian all-too-often exhorts. This is not
the proper choice and, to say the least, it is an
incredible and gross oversimplification, indeed a distorted

view, and an unjustifiable affront both to human intellect and to academically informed biblical scholarship. According to this scholarship, the Bible contains a mixture of myth and actual historical fact. It has been one of the most important contributions of contemporary scholarship to have made much headway in sorting out what is myth and what is fact, and just as importantly, to have clearly defined the religious truths which are embedded in the myths.

For Christianity to remain relevant to society (or, as some would say, to regain its relevance), it must be continually open to new insights and to the new scholarship which is based upon ongoing research not only in theology but in the physical sciences. The biblical story of the "fall" most surely contains religious truth (for example, that we human beings are flawed, inadequate and somehow unable and unwilling to live up to our full potential, etc.); yet taken literally, this story is (as John Hick has pointed out) not only scientifically but morally and logically objectionable:

> we know today that the conditions that were to cause human disease and mortality and the necessity for man to undertake the perils of hunting and the labours of agriculture and building, were already part of the natural order prior to the emergence of man and prior therefore to any first human sin, as were also the conditions causing such further 'evils' as earthquake, storm, flood, drought, and plague. And second, the policy of punishing the whole succeeding human race for the sin of the first human pair is, by the best human moral standards, unjust and does not provide anything that can be recognized by these standards as a theodicy.

Third, there is a basic and fatal incoherence at
the heart of the mythically based 'solution'.
The Creator is preserved from any responsibility
for the existence of evil by the claim that He
made men (or angels) as free and finitely perfect
creatures, happy in the knowledge of Himself, and
subject to no strains or temptations, but that
they themselves inexplicably and inexcusably
rebelled against Him. But this suggestion
amounts to a sheer self-contradiction. It is
impossible to conceive of wholly good beings in a
wholly good world becoming sinful. To say that
they do is to postulate the self-creation of evil
ex nihilo.[22]

The myth of the "fall" can only be saved by the addition
(as can be seen, for example, in the thought of Augustine
and Calvin) of the highly questionable doctrine of an
absolute divine predestination to explain why a perfect
creation would sin. But, as Hick contends,

this in turn only leads the theodicy to
contradict itself. For its original intention
was to blame evil upon the misuse of creaturely
free will. But now this misuse is itself said to
fall under the divine predestinating decrees.
Thus the theodicy collapses into radical
incoherence, and its more persistent defenders
have become involved in ever more desperate and
implausible epicycles of theory to save it.[23]

SATAN

Equally problematic is the literal interpretation of
biblical passages which attribute evil and suffering to
evil powers, notably to Satan and his cohorts.[24]   To

commit one's faith to a literal interpretation of these passages seems tragically misguided and uninformed. Belief in the actual physical existence of Satan would certainly enable one to account for much of the world's evil, to be sure, yet academic theologians increasingly have come to regard Satan not as an actual personal being, but as a symbolic representation of the evil inherent in the world. If, on the other hand, Satan were actually to exist and act as he is portrayed in the biblical accounts and in the writings and folklore of the subsequent tradition, certain theological problems would arise, problems for which there appear to be no convincing answers. How, for example, could Satan as an archangel, supposedly created wholly good and in the immediate presence of God, rebel against God? As was the case with regard to the "fall" of Adam, subsequent theological reflection had little choice in the answering of this question except to postulate a divine predestination for Satan's fall.[25] But there are no convincing reasons given as to why God would do such a thing.[26] Many biblical passages, to be sure, assume that Satan's activity is controlled by God for the achievement of divine ends.[27] One recent commentator acknowledges, accordingly, that "it would be utterly out of harmony with the New Testament to concede to the devil and the powers of evil certain autonomous spheres not subject to God, where they can reign and hold sway as sovereign."[28] Paul, for example, attributes his own sufferings to Satan's messenger, in accord with God's wish to guard him against undue exaltation (2 Cor 12:7); suffering "produces repentance that leads to salvation" (2 Cor 7:10). But if this is the case, if Satan's activity is entirely in accord with God's will and plan, the problem which arises is to explain how this activity is consistent with an

all-powerful and all-loving Being. The belief that evil is
attributable to Satan seems, in fact, superfluous, for the
underlying question remains: why does God--through Satan
or otherwise--permit such evil?

DIVINE POWER AND CREATURELY FREE WILL

Many Christians, nevertheless, continue to put their
faith and trust in the Bible as a literal account of the
origin and meaning of evil, despite the fact that such a
position is difficult to support intellectually not only
for the reasons already suggested, but because the Bible,
quite simply, does not offer a single, unified and coherent
account of the meaning of evil and its relationship to
God. One major biblical strand attributes evil to divine
causality, either directly or through agents such as Satan,
while another equally central strand (if not
quantitatively, at least doctrinally) attributes evil to
human free will.[29] God's sole responsibility is clearly
attested to in passages like the following: "Does evil
befall a city, unless the Lord has done it?" (Amos 3:6);
"Is it not from the mouth of the Most High that good and
evil come?" (Lam 3:38); "I form light and create darkness,
I make weal and create woe, I am the Lord, who do all these
things" (Isa 45:7); God, we are told, "has mercy upon
whomsoever he wills, and he hardens the heart of whomsoever
he wills" (Rom 9:18); and even Jesus' crucifixion is said
to have happened "according to the definite plan and
foreknowledge of God" (Acts 4:28). Human beings, we are
told, furthermore, are either "vessels of wrath made for
destruction" or "vessels of mercy" which God "has prepared
beforehand for glory" (Rom 9:22-23). And yet, despite such
teachings, other passages suggest that it is not God, but
we ourselves who in fact are responsible for our acts, for

otherwise it would make no sense for God to reward or
punish us. Paul warns, for example, that some will be cut
off from the tree of salvation if they do not remain
steadfast (Rom 11:22-23), and we are told that Christians
must "work out" their own salvation. God works in us by
"inspiring" (rather than coercing) us "both in will and
deed, for his own chosen purpose" (Phil 2:12).

THE MYSTERY OF EVIL

In light of such paradoxical and seemingly
contradictory teachings about evil and its relationship to
God, it is hardly surprising that several biblical passages
discourage us from seeking a comprehensive solution to the
problem of evil. "Woe to him who strives with his maker,
an earthen vessel with the potter! Does the clay say to
him who fashions it, 'What are you making'? or 'Your work
has no handles'?" (Isa 45:9). "Who is this," God demands
of Job out of the whirlwind, "that darkens counsel by words
without knowledge?" (Job 38:2). And as Job came to
acknowledge, Paul proclaims "the depth of the riches and
wisdom and knowledge of God! How unsearchable are his
judgments and how inscrutable his ways!" (Rom 11:33). We
are encouraged to cultivate a trusting faith in the divine
plan; all evil is reconcilable with God's providential
will, though his plan is clearly beyond human
comprehension.[30]

Many Christians would leave the matter here. And
yet, as was noted above, the faith solution not only has
serious negative implications, but is simply not a viable
option for many people: the devastating reality of evil
in their lives (or in the world at large) renders such
faith impossible. For growing numbers of reflective
Christians, furthermore, it has become increasingly

important to "think through" their religious beliefs and to
seek at least some semblance of rational understanding as
an essential underpinning of their faith. They refuse to
abdicate their reasoning abilities, and it is simply not
acceptable for them to acquiesce unquestioningly to the
paradoxical biblical explanations as the final and complete
word on the matter. The conception of God as somehow
controlling all events has emerged as a particularly
problematic issue (due in part, though by no means
exclusively, to the efforts of process thinkers), for it
appears to render human freedom and moral responsibility an
illusion; and this is counterintuitive, for we know that we
are free. Indeed, if we were not free, God would be a
great deceiver and, as such, hardly the all-loving being
which alone is worthy of our worship.

A NEW THEISM

At this point, we would do well to consider the fact
that our understanding of God has undergone a continual,
dynamic evolution, and that the future (or present)
viability of our religious tradition may well depend upon
our willingness to remain open to further insights. As a
species we have moved from primitive animistic beliefs to
what (presumably) is a more viable comprehension of the
absolute and ultimate reality which western theology calls
"God."[31] Much of the biblical and traditional Christian
understanding of God depends upon a particular world view:
God is modeled largely on the patriarchal ruler of the
clan, and later upon Roman and Greek rulers.[32] At its
worst, he is seen as a Zeus-like figure who controls events
on earth as pawns in a chess game. Yet, of course, this
view is no longer adequate; our twentieth century world
view no longer attributes all earthly events to a divine

being (or beings), but rather to human and physical causes. To continue to conceptualize God in terms of the ancient cosmology, accordingly, is surely inappropriate and, I would suggest, harmful. For unless our understanding of God is immediately coherent with our world view, it runs the risk of becoming irrelevant and the object of ridicule. "We are," as one modern theologian who is sensitive to this point informs us, "forced to recognize that the form of theism which most Western men have taken for granted and have by and large made use of to explicate their understanding of faith in God is now widely held to be anything but reasonable."[33] Many contemporary theologians now agree that our religious faith "is molded, in the form we know it, by a cast of thought that belongs to a past age."[34] Perhaps no one has addressed this point more forcefully and constructively than Whitehead. He has drawn our attention to the crucial (yet often overlooked) point that with each major advance in science, not only is our world view somewhat modified, but so too must our religious beliefs be modified:

> Religion will not regain its old power until it can face change in the same spirit as does science. Its principles may be eternal, but the expression of those principles requires continual development. This evolution of religion is in the main a disengagement of its own proper ideas from the adventitious notions which have crept into it by reason of the expression of its own ideas in terms of the imaginative picture of the world entertained in previous ages . . . . The great point to be kept in mind is that normally an advance in science will show that statements of various religious beliefs require some sort of modification.[35]

With the advances in modern science, accordingly, to say nothing of the insights of modern biblical scholarship, we now can appreciate the fact that much of what the Bible understands about God, about evil, and about the world's creation, etc., can no longer be taken literally as the final word on these matters. Obviously, the earth cannot be seen as the static center of the entire universe, nor can we continue to believe that the species were created in their present forms "all at once" during the first week of creation. Current scientific theories have no place for an historical Adam and Eve, and while the Genesis account of the first human pair continues (and rightly so) to have great religious significance—for it conveys its author's religious insights about the origin and meaning of evil—the account can no longer be interpreted as historical fact. To place one's faith in this story as the main explanation for the world's evil is no longer prudent. Nor is it prudent to continue to commit one's faith to the belief that all things are controlled according to God's will and plan, that "no purpose of thine can be thwarted" (Job 42:2), or to the belief that evil is caused by God's direct agency (through Satan or otherwise) as punishment, as a warning, or a test of faith, etc. Jesus revealed a very different vision of God: a loving, persuasive agent, not a coercive, all-determining and all-controlling force. This vision is the central focus of the process thought to be considered in this book, and its implications for the problem of evil, as we shall see, are immense.

Chapter 3: RATIONAL SOLUTIONS

The alternative to simply accepting in faith that all things happen because of God's incomprehensible will and plan, and that the Bible's explanations for evil are to be accepted literally and unquestioningly, is to seek intellectually viable explanations, "theodicies," for the world's evil and its relationship to God. Christian theologians over the centuries have, of course, formulated a variety of such explanations to account for both the moral evil which afflicts us (sin, greed, envy, hate, deceit, etc.) and the physical evil in the world which causes so much suffering (pain, disease, deformity, famines, etc.).[36] Yet, interestingly enough, many of the traditional theodicies are in fact defences of several biblical explanations for evil. While it may be the case that increasingly fewer theologians insist upon the rational viability of the "fall" story in Genesis or the attribution of evil to Satan, evil is still commonly attributed to the misguided use of human free will (without necessarily referring to an historical "fall")--the so-called free will solution; and evil is still explained as God's will and plan: it is attributed to divine punishment, to a test of faith or a warning, given by God; and so on (as we shall see).

To refer to all of these as "rational" explanations for evil will perhaps not immediately seem justifiable, for sceptics and atheists could argue with some validity that

"rational" explanations for evil ought not to assume that
God exists (for it is this very point which is at issue),
but rather ought to explain evil without reference to a God
or gods. There are explanations of this kind[37]--evil,
for example, is explained as the by-product of natural laws
which have evolved through time and which in themselves are
an absolute necessity for the world to exist as an orderly,
coherent system; yet the issue we are addressing in this
book is the problem within the Christian theistic system of
reconciling the world's evil with belief in an
omnibenevolent and all-powerful God. The issue, then, is
not how rationally to explain evil without reference to
God, but to assess the rational viability (the inner
coherence, etc.) of the proposed explanations for evil
vis-à-vis the conception of God espoused by Christianity
and vis-à-vis our contemporary world view.[38] In this
context, however, the point which process thinkers
emphatically make is that many of the traditional
theodicies, biblically based or otherwise, are rationally
indefensible since they employ an invalid conception of
God, a conception which gives rise to various
contradictions, and which is counterintuitive to our
religious sensibilities and to our contemporary world
view. If the traditional God is immutably unaffected by
the world and coercively all-determining, as process
thinkers suggest, implying that he either directly causes
all evils for a variety of reasons (evils are tests of
faith, warnings, punishments, etc.), or at least that he
permits them when he could have prevented them, then there
would seem to be little hope for a viable explanation for
evil vis-à-vis such a God.

In the previous chapter we considered two of the
main explanations for evil utilized in biblical thought and

in the subsequent Christian tradition: the "fall" of Adam
and the sinister meddling of Satan. And while this
discussion took place in the context of the faith solution
(and the issue of biblical literalism), I think it is fair
to say that the discussion has relevance also for the
closely related issue we are now addressing: the rational
viability of such explanations. The "fall" of Adam as the
cause of evil, as we noted, has serious scientific, moral
and logical deficiencies which count decisively against its
rational viability; and likewise the attribution of evil to
Satan seems inconsistent with belief in a good and powerful
God, and leaves the essential problem of evil unresolved.
But let us turn to a brief discussion of some of the other
biblically based explanations which also have been utilized
heavily in traditional theological writings. My intention
is to discuss these theories merely in brief and, as such,
I make no claims to doing full justice to their complexity
and subtlety of detail and context. And yet, I trust that
my simplified treatment is neither inaccurate nor
misleading. My purpose is to point out some of the main
objections to these theories, particularly from the
perspective of process theodicy.

THE FREE WILL EXPLANATION

Moral evil has generally been attributed to the
conscious free will decisions of human beings--an
explanation which, however, need not necessarily be
associated with the Adamic myth of the "fall." We have the
ability to choose between good and evil, it is argued, and
evil arises from our wrong choices, or at least from
choices which bring about less good than is possible in any
given situation. Moral evil, then, is caused by human
beings, not by God, and it is believed to be far better to

have the freedom to decide our own acts than to have no
freedom at all. Otherwise, we would be mere automata,
determined either by God or by the efficient causality of
the world. A recent defender of this explanation, Alvin
Plantinga, summarizes it as follows:

> A world containing creatures who are
> significantly free (and freely perform more good
> than evil actions) is more valuable, all else
> being equal, than a world containing no free
> creatures at all. Now God can create free
> creatures, but He can't <u>cause</u> or <u>determine</u> them
> to do only what is right. For if He does so,
> then they aren't significantly free after all;
> they do not do what is right <u>freely</u>. To create
> creatures capable of <u>moral good</u>, therefore, He
> must create creatures capable of moral evil; and
> He can't give these creatures the freedom to
> perform evil and at the same time prevent them
> from doing so. As it turned out, sadly enough,
> some of the free creatures God created went wrong
> in the exercise of their freedom; this is the
> source of moral evil. The fact that free
> creatures sometimes go wrong, however, neither
> counts against God's omnipotence nor against His
> goodness; for He could have forestalled the
> occurrence of moral evil only by removing the
> possibility of moral good.[39]

But there are a number of critical questions which
have been raised about this explanation, questions which
focus especially upon the "free will--determinism"
debate[40] and the contention that the traditional
Christian conception of God is inconsistent with creaturely
freedom. (As we have seen, many biblical passages portray

an almost fatalistic conception of the all-determining will of God, and this belief has remained strong throughout Christian history. In Chapter 7 we shall note its use in the writings of such major theologians as Augustine, Aquinas, Luther and Calvin). Process thinkers defend, with some justification, the reality of creaturely freedom versus an absolute causal determinism of physical causes, yet they vigorously concur with the critique regarding the inconsistency of traditional theism vis-à-vis creaturely free will. In a later chapter (Chapter 8) we shall examine the process thinkers' defence of the free will explanation and assess its viability vis-à-vis their reconstructed conception of God as a persuasive "lure" (versus the coercive, all-determining divine power which they take to be implied by the traditional theism).

EVIL AS GOD'S PUNISHMENT

While traditional Christianity attributes moral evil to the misuse of human free will, there are several explanations for physical evil which have persisted strongly since biblical times. One such explanation is that evil is God's punishment for our sinful abuse of free will. The fact that our word "pain" is derived from the Latin word "poena," meaning "punishment," is not coincidental,[41] but can be attributed to the predominance of the view that pain is given to us directly by God as punishment.[42] God punishes Adam and Eve for their sin, Adam with laborious work and Eve with childbearing pain (Gen 3:16-19), and later destroys much of the world with the great flood, as punishment for human sinfulness (Gen 6-9). The success or failure of Israel's crops and her battles, moreover, was interpreted as either divine punishments or blessings. Jeremiah, for example, attributes the fall of Jerusalem to sin: "This calamity has come upon you because you burnt these sacrifices and sinned against the Lord and did not obey the Lord or conform to his laws, statutes, and teachings" (Jer 44: 22-23). The "comforters" of Job, likewise, assure him that his suffering is due to God's punishment: "For consider, what innocent man has ever perished? Where have you seen the upright destroyed? This I know, that those who plough mischief and sow trouble reap as they have sown" (Job 4:7-8).

This explanation for evil can readily be seen also in the New Testament writings, although it does not seem to be quite so dominant there.[43] According to Paul, "a man reaps what he sows" (Gal 6:7-8), and Matthew informs us that the poor tree which yields bad fruit "is cut down and burnt" (Mt 7:18-19); those who do not do the will of God are cut off (Mt 7:21); the sheep will be separated from the goats (Mt 25:31-46); and so on. In the post-biblical centuries, this belief once again became a dominant one, due as much as anything (I would imagine) to the especially high profile it was given in the greatly influential theology of St. Augustine. "Free will," he informs us, "is the cause of our doing evil and thy [God's] just judgment is the cause of our having to suffer from its consequences." Likewise, John Calvin, among many others, taught that all the calamities which overtake us are to be attributed to divine chastisements.[44] The much discussed Lisbon earthquake of 1755, to cite a random historical example, was universally regarded as an act of divine wrath, as were the wars fought throughout the centuries. Abraham Lincoln's second inaugural address, for example, attributes the immense suffering endured during the American Civil War to God's punishment for America's

enslavement of the black man. In a similar vein, some
Jewish theologians attributed the holocaust of the Second
World War to God's chastisement of his chosen people![45]
And in the minds of the masses of contemporary Christians,
there seems to be continued and passionate support for this
belief: God punishes the wicked and rewards the good; all
events in this life are regarded as somehow in accord with
God's plan; all things are God's blessings or curses.[46]

This explanation for evil has, of course, not gone
unchallenged. There are in fact, and most interestingly
so, explicit biblical passages which reject it. The author
of the Book of Job, for example, clearly repudiates the
idea that evil is the direct result of divine punishment,
as does the author of Ecclesiastes who assures us that "the
same fate befalls everyone, just and unjust alike, good and
bad, clean and unclean" (Eccles 9:2). The Gospel of
Matthew, likewise, states that God "makes his sun rise on
good and bad alike, and sends rain on the honest and the
dishonest" (Mt 5:45). And Luke writes of Jesus' apparent
rejection of the punishment teaching: after hearing of the
deaths of some Galileans at the hands of Pilate, Jesus
responded by asking: "Do you imagine that, because these
Galileans suffered this fate, they must have been greater
sinners than anyone else in Galilee? I tell you they were
not . . . . Or the eighteen people who were killed when
the tower fell on them . . . . do you imagine they were
more guilty than all the other people living in Jerusalem?
I tell you they were not" (Lk 13:1-3).[47]

There are, furthermore, many post-biblical
repudiations of the divine punishment theory. Theists and
atheists alike have rejected this explanation for evil as
thoroughly inconsistent with belief in an all-loving God.
Process thinkers agree. There is no justification for

attributing such evils to God, and indeed, to do so seems
to be a blasphemous denial of the divine benevolence.
Granted, there must be a balance between God's love and his
justice, yet to attribute physical evils to divine justice
seems to bespeak of a rather primitive conception of God,
one which is, according to process thinkers, a serious
misunderstanding of divine power and divine causal agency
in the world. If God were to coercively intervene in the
affairs of human beings to punish and reward, would this
not be inconsistent with the reality of genuine creaturely
autonomy vis-à-vis God?[48] According to process thinkers,
God operates continually, yet solely persuasively, within
each creature, "luring" it toward the actualization of
whatever good is possible in any given situation. The
creature, however, may or may not accept this lure (see
below, Part Two); God, in short, does not coercively
intervene.

The explanation for evil as divine punishment,
moreover, has little rational support when one considers
the empirical evidence.[49] There is, quite simply, no
convincing data for such a view; it cannot be shown that
physical evil is directly attributable to divine punishment
for moral wrongs. And, indeed, the distribution of
physical evils is far too arbitrary and unjust to believe
that they are given by a benevolent God. The empirical
evidence in fact would seem to favor the view that the
physical evils we suffer have physical causes: cancers are
caused by breathing too much polluted air, or by eating too
much red meat, and so on. There is no justification for
attributing such horrors to God.[50]

EVIL AS GOD'S WARNING OR A TEST OF FAITH

A closely related explanation for evil espoused in
the biblical literature and in much of Christianity

throughout the centuries is the view that <u>evil</u> <u>is</u> <u>a</u> <u>warning</u>
or <u>a</u> <u>test</u> <u>of</u> <u>faith</u> <u>given</u> <u>by</u> <u>God</u> explicitly for these
purposes.   Physical afflictions and natural disasters,
accordingly, are believed to serve

> a moral end which compensates the physical evil
> which they cause. The awful nature of these
> phenomena [natural disasters], the overwhelming
> power of the forces at work, and man's
> helplessness before them, rouse him from the
> religious indifference to which he is so prone.
> They inspire a reverential awe of the Creator who
> made them, and controls them, and a salutary fear
> of violating the laws which He has imposed.[51]

This certainly was the case with Job, whose physical
torments were a test of his faith and which served the
moral end, if not of bringing him back to the path of
righteousness--for he was (according to the text) already
righteous--at   least   of   bringing   him   to   a   clear
acknowledgement of God's great power and glory, and to a
strengthening of his powers of resistance and faith.
Likewise, Paul sees suffering as a test of faith (2 Cor
8:2) [52] and a call to remain patient and steadfast: "Let
hope keep you joyful; in trouble stand firm; persist in
prayer" (Rom 12:12); "Out of darkness let light shine" (2
Cor 4:6). Suffering, according to the author of the First
Letter of Peter, similarly, is seen as a test of faith,
much as gold is tested as it "passes through the assayer's
fire;" likewise do "trials come so that your faith may
prove itself worthy of all praise, glory, and honour when
Jesus Christ is revealed" (1 Peter 1:6-7).   The Old
Testament reference for this is Proverbs 17:3 (among
others): "The melting-pot is for silver and the crucible
for gold, but it is the Lord who assays the hearts of

men."[53]

This explanation for evil has, like the others we
have discussed, met with justifiable resistance. For while
it may be the case that those who suffer can use that
suffering to strengthen their faith or to bring them back
to the path of righteousness, to believe that God directly
causes suffering for these reasons is surely to put belief
in divine benevolence to the test! It is also a
misunderstanding of divine power, as the process thinkers
point out, to conceptualize God's causal agency as
manipulating earthly events for this or any other reason.
It can be argued, further, that even if God did impose
suffering as goads to turn people to him, it is just as
likely to be the case that the suffering will turn people
away from him. The contemporary philosopher H. J.
McCloskey makes this point quite unequivocally: "if God's
object in bringing about natural calamities [or other types
of suffering] is to inspire reverence and awe, He is a
bungler. There are many more reliable methods of achieving
this end."[54] Surely an omnibenevolent God would use a
less harsh method to bring his people to him. Indeed, we
must ask why God would find such tests of faith even to be
necessary, given the traditional conception of God as
immutably and eternally omniscient. Would he not already
know how the afflicted person would react before he is so
afflicted? It is, according to process thinkers, a rather
primitive conception of God to believe that he sends tests
and warnings to his people to discover whether or not they
will remain steadfast or to return them to the path of
righteousness, or for whatever reason. Theology can and
must do better than this![55]

SUFFERING FOR OTHERS

Another biblical theory which has an especially predominant role in the New Testament is the view that suffering can contribute to the good of others. Inspired by Isaiah 40-55 and in particular the Servant Songs (Isa 42:1-4; 49:1-6; 50:4-9; 52:13-53:12), many New Testament passages espouse the view that "our suffering may be part of God's work in the world to do some greater good for other people."[56] The prime example of this, of course, is the suffering of Jesus. Just as the suffering of the Jews during the exile had to be explained as due to something other than punishment--for Israel had "received at the Lord's hand double measure for all her sins" (Isa 40:2), so, likewise, Jesus' suffering had to be explained otherwise than as punishment for his sins. His suffering was, in fact, explained as a necessity on behalf of the sins of others.[57] Accordingly, to be a Christian, a follower of Christ, means to share in his suffering, to suffer for others as he did. This view is evident in the Gospel writings and even more so in the letters of Paul. Jesus' followers must "drink of the cup" and "be baptised with the baptism" with which Jesus was baptised (Mk 10: 38-39), signifying that they will suffer as did Jesus.[58] The followers of Christ must "carry his cross" of pain and suffering (Lk 14:27), not just in drastic situations (martyrdom and the like) but "daily," in everyday events. Likewise, "Paul sees in Christ that one who, like Adam, in universal scope determines the destiny of humanity and through his eschatological suffering and dying also places his followers in the 'fellowship of his sufferings.' The 'sufferings of Christ' of the Christians signify not only their belonging to Christ, but also the eschatological efficacy and impact of his death."[59]

This view has undeniable and obvious worth in helping Christ's followers cope with suffering, but it seems to me that it is far less useful as a means of explaining suffering. Why an all-powerful and all-loving God would cause or permit suffering remains unanswered. Process thinkers, furthermore, would protest that it is unacceptable to believe that God would inflict suffering on his creatures for any reason, including that which sees it as somehow benefiting others. If this is in fact what the traditional theology holds, then it seems that such a belief is an invalid understanding of the divine causal agency in the world. The suffering has naturalistic explanations, and while one can use one's suffering for the benefit of others (although how one does this is far from clear)[60] it surely is inadequate, if not blasphemous, to attribute the suffering to God.

FURTHER EXPLANATIONS FOR EVIL

Besides these biblically based explanations for evil, there are a number of explanations which are not biblically based but which have long been utilized by Christian theologians. I do not propose to deal with all of these in detail, but wish merely to refer to the main points of some of them--in particular, those which play a significant role also in process theodicy: evil as the by-product of natural laws, the character-building or soul-making theory, and the ultimate harmony or aesthetic theory.

Physical evil is explained, first of all, as the necessary and inevitable by-product of natural laws, laws which are themselves absolutely essential for there to be a world order.[61] Process thinkers would agree, and yet they do not support the traditional doctrine of the creation of the world by God ex nihilo, or the belief that God need not have created this particular world with its particular laws (or indeed any world at all). The position of process thinkers is that some world necessarily exists, if only a primordial chaos of matter or energy. For the sake of aesthetic value, however, (see below) God chose to "lure" the chaos into an ordered world, rather than simply leaving it as a mere, unstructured randomness. But with the ordering of the world, evil and discord necessarily have arisen, for the laws of nature which structure the world also cause suffering. The water which sustains life, for example, can drown us, to say nothing of the suffering caused by the interlocking predatory chain whereby species live by killing one other, etc.

Protests at this point that God could have (and ought to have) created a world with less opportunity for discord and evil, and failing this to have created no world at all, are rejected by process thinkers. They insist, among other things, that a utopian paradise of perfect creatures in a perfect world is a meaningless notion. Human beings cannot simply be given (that is, be created with) morally virtuous characters, but must slowly develop their moral and spiritual (as well as their physical and mental) natures.

There may appear to be some similarity between this explanation for evil (as the necessary by-product of natural laws) and the ancient "principle of plenitude" utilized by Plato, Augustine, Aquinas and a host of others throughout the centuries. Yet process thinkers would hardly support the central contention of the principle of plenitude which holds that God created all possible levels of beings, leaving no gaps in the hierarchy from lowly, inert matter to the heights of the heavenly realms. This

principle attributes evil to the fact that with the
creation of this "great chain of being"[62] some levels are
more perfect than others.   Augustine, for example,
explains that "from things earthly to things heavenly, from
the visible to the invisible, there are some things better
than others; and for this purpose are they unequal, in
order that they might all exist."[63] Aquinas agrees: "It
pertains to divine providence that the grades of being
which are possible are fulfilled," and some things will
necessarily be better than others;   that is, since some
will have the power to fall from the good.[64]   This
explanation for evil is rejected by process thinkers (and
others) for a number of reasons, not the least of which is
that there is simply no evidence that all levels of being
have, in fact, been created. The principle of plenitude,
furthermore, is based on a static conception of reality
which is at odds with current evolutionary theory.[65]

Process thinkers, nevertheless, would find Austin
Farrer's use of this principle more acceptable: the view
that physical evils result from a "mutual interference of
systems."[66]   Creatures (both   inorganic and   organic)
inevitably interfere with one another, since what is good
and necessary for one creature causes suffering and discord
in others. The process version of this is that every act
and decision of every creature has repercussions in the
immediate environment of that creature, and that with every
new possibility actualized by each creature, other possible
values are lost.[67] To eliminate the evil of loss and of
interference, God would have to eliminate the world itself
from which this evil arises: there simply can be no world
without such evil. And if one asks why God then did not
create only spiritual beings (angels) and thereby
effectively have avoided the entire realm of physical

matter and its discord, the process thinkers' response
would be that God seeks significant experiences and values,
and that these cannot be attained merely from spiritual
"yes-men"[68] (nor indeed, for that matter, from a state of
unstructured, random chaos).

But let us turn to another of the traditional
theories that seeks to explain evil and its relationship to
God: the character-building theory.[69] Human beings, it
is argued, cannot have been created wholly virtuous or
perfect, but rather must struggle with evil in order to
acquire morally good characters. John Hick refers to this
as "soul-making" (a term first used by the poet Keats, but
which has a long history within Christian thought). Hick's
contention is that the creation of human beings is a
two-fold process: the first stage resulted in the creation
of physical matter and in the evolutionary development of
the human species, while the second stage is one in which
human beings have the opportunity to spiritually perfect
themselves.[70] Process thinkers would agree with Hick's
further contention that God could not have created a world
free of pain and suffering and yet which was populated by
significantly free and autonomous creatures. For according
to process thinkers, all creatures must necessarily have
some independence and autonomy which God cannot overrule,
if they are to remain creatures. Any world populated by
creatures, accordingly, will inevitably contain evil, for
creaturely freedom can cause evil as well as good. Process
thinkers argue, however, that while our moral and spiritual
potentialities can only be actualized through overcoming
pain and affliction, any hint that such pain and evil is
given by God directly for this soul-making purpose is an
unacceptable denial of divine benevolence and a
misunderstanding of the divine omnipotent causal

agency.[71] Physical evils arise from the creativity of
creatures and from the natural laws which are necessary for
the world to exist. There is no justification in blaming
specific evils on the direct causal agency of God. There
is, at any rate, a far too unfair distribution of evils to
believe that God has deliberately distributed them
according to a benevolent will and plan. And indeed, not
all evils seem to serve the moral end of soul-making: some
appear to be merely gratuitous and some so abundant and
overwhelming that the sufferer succumbs to them, resulting
thereby not in greater moral perfection but in devastated
lives.[72]

   A final aspect of the traditional theodicy to be
considered is the aesthetic understanding of evil, the
so-called ultimate harmony solution, which holds that the
world as a whole is good, and that evil is a necessary part
of the perfect, overall harmony. What seems to be evil to
us is in fact, from God's perfect perspective, really a
good, since it is either a necessary part of a good whole
or (in another version) a necessary means to a good
end.[73] Process thinkers, however, do not regard the
world as a perfect whole, with all evil and discord serving
some good end which apparently has been ordained by God's
incomprehensible will and plan. Much evil may be simply
gratuitous (yet, see below) and much leads not to good ends
but to even greater evils. Indeed, to argue that all evils
serve a good end is in effect to deny the reality of evil
as evil: it becomes an illusion, for what seems to be
evil is really a good in disguise! If, on the other hand,
we do interpret such evil as evil (and this is far more
generally the case) human rationality is jeopardized, since
from God's perspective our concepts of good and evil are
invalid. While it is obvious that our perspective is

finite, limited, and incomplete, yet, if from God's perfect view our concepts of good and evil are simply mistaken, then surely rationality ceases. "We are asked," in effect, "to accept a higher morality out of devotion and total ignorance . . . . We are asked . . . to forget the little we know of right and wrong, abdicate our intelligence, [and] submit ourselves to something we know not of."[74]

There are other problems with the aesthetic theory. If evil is part of a good whole or a means to a good end, does this not render misguided and simply mistaken any efforts to eradicate it? And must we not, then, cease to work toward the creation of a more just society, a society with less of the evil and suffering caused by injustice, poverty, exploitation and a number of other apparently amendable causes? Yet, can we really regard earthly events like the holocaust and the starvation of millions of people as part of a good whole or as a means to a good end? Process thinkers would find such a view absolutely contradictory to belief in a benevolent God and a serious misunderstanding of his causal agency to think that he has planned, caused or permitted (when he could have prevented) such evil, for any purpose. Even a post mortem heavenly realm could not explain, undo, compensate, or justify the evils suffered by countless innocent souls, in particular those of children. "The price that is paid for long run good is too high. . . . The end does not justify the means."[75] Despite the common view that a heavenly realm is necessary to somehow amend the excessive, undeserved and debilitating evils suffered by human beings, Dostoevski's point seems to hold: nothing can amend such suffering, and a God who would cause or permit it (for whatever reasons) is not a benevolent God.[76]

Process thinkers, nevertheless, do utilize a version
of the aesthetic theory which they believe is less
problematic. They regard evil as inevitable and necessary
in the slow but steady advance toward ever greater levels
of intensity and harmony--that is, in the acquiring of
aesthetic value--in the experiences of human beings, an
aesthetic advance which is necessary for life to
continue.[77] Human beings require experiences which
maintain the "aesthetic mean" between too much order and
too much disorder, and also between too much complexity and
too much triviality. An ordered, utopic paradise is not a
suitable environment for significant human life (and
indeed human life could hardly exist in such an
environment, since it is difficult to see how moral good
could be applicable to beings which have nothing to
overcome, nothing against which to contest, etc.). An
ordered utopia would be one of monotony and triviality, one
of too little complexity--in short, one in which the
necessary aesthetic value would be lacking. "A too tame
and harmless order and a too wild and dangerous . . .
disorder--these are the evils to be maximally avoided in
some golden mean."[78]

Chapter 4: PROCESS THEODICY

The main argument set forth by process thinkers against the traditional explanations for evil, as we have noted, centers about the traditional conception of God's power. Not all Christian theologians, of course, over the past twenty centuries have conceived God in a uniform manner;[79] yet, as process theologian David Griffin has argued in great detail, the central "notion in the traditional idea of God in Western thought has been the notion that God controls, or at least could control, every detail of the events in the world."[80] And whether he directly causes events or merely permits them, the result is the same: events occur only if they are in accord with his will. The fact that God can apparently overrule creaturely autonomy at any time leaves little doubt that he can totally determine events. Such a God has a virtual "monopoly of decision-making,"[81] according to Hartshorne, and presumably can prevent anything undesirable from occurring by performing "miraculous" interventions. He wills both goods and evils for his creatures--the goods as blessings and the evils, as we have seen, for a number of supposedly legitimate reasons--as punishments, tests of faith, and so on. Griffin's study has shown--to my mind, convincingly--that the dominant theologians of the Christian tradition have, in fact, shared this common belief in God's power as all-pervasive (despite inevitable nuances and differing emphases), and that such an understanding of divine power renders problematic any

genuine creaturely autonomy.[82] The writings of Luther
and Calvin, for example, are quite clear in their
insistence upon a complete divine determinism of events,
and while Calvin also insists that human beings are
responsible, nevertheless, for their sinful acts, this
seems to be a "purely verbal" claim which is negated by the
conception of God he espouses.[83] It is much the same in
the greatly influential writings of Aquinas. He contends,
for example, that God is the "primary" cause of all events,
while creatures are the "secondary" causes. The logic of
this argument, as we shall see, is rejected by process
thinkers as thoroughly invalid, for it is likewise a merely
verbal assertion of creaturely freedom, an assertion which
seems to be rendered invalid by the doctrine of God
espoused by Aquinas.[84]

Process thinkers contend that the traditional
conception of God's power (and equally invalid conceptions
of other divine attributes--omniscience, immutability, and
the like) renders the theodicy question problematic, if not
virtually unsolvable. Creaturely free will and moral
responsibility for evil surely are undermined by a God who
causes all events, regardless of his reasons for doing
so--as punishments, tests, warnings, etc.--and regardless
of whether he causes the events directly or through
secondary agents. Creaturely freedom is undermined also by
a God who intervenes periodically to effect his will on
worldly affairs, to eradicate certain evils, for example.
Such interventions, which when seen by us are called
"miracles," would violate natural laws and supersede
creaturely autonomy (at least temporarily). The fact that
God intervenes intermittently would, furthermore, raise the
question as to why he has not prevented more of the world's
most ghastly evils. Are we to believe that all of the

evils which remain have a specific meaning and purpose within the divine plan?   Such a view would certainly be consistent with the belief that God controls everything that happens according to his providential will and plan, but does this not render any genuine creaturely autonomy vis-à-vis this God virtually unreal?   Creatures, it seems, would be permitted to act freely only if their acts were in accordance with God's will.

If this is in fact what the traditional theism implies—and, to be sure, for some this assessment is debatable—then it would appear that the objections of process thinkers have some validity.   Creaturely free will would be unreal vis-à-vis such a God, and yet if creatures are not free and morally responsible for their acts and decisions, it is difficult to consider them creatures at all, rather than merely attributes of God's all-pervasive being.   It is equally difficult to justify the belief that evils are to be attributed to God's punishments, tests, warnings, etc., when creatures have no freedom and no moral responsibility for their actions vis-à-vis such a God.   To believe that God causes evils (or permits them through Satan or other secondary causes) as punishments or tests, seems to be a clear misunderstanding of divine power which contradicts genuine creaturely freedom.   It is difficult, furthermore, to believe in an afterlife existence where earthly goods and evils will be rewarded or punished, for if creatures are not responsible for their earthly acts, they hardly merit either rewards or punishments.

AN OUTLINE OF PARTS TWO AND THREE

In the pages to follow, I wish to examine the contributions of process thought, represented mainly by

Hartshorne, to the theodicy issue. Part Two will focus upon his reconstructed doctrine of God. In place of the God of traditional Christianity, a God which process thinkers define as "monopolar," statically immutable and independent of the world, process theism conceives God as "dipolar," dynamic and processive. Divine knowledge and power, for example, are conceived as partially dependent upon the acts and decisions of the world's free creatures; God does not know or cause all things from some nontemporal, eternal realm, but knows all that is actual as actual and all that is possible as possible. He does not coercively predetermine or control creaturely acts and decisions, nor does he coercively intervene in creaturely affairs. Rather, he "persuasively" lures his creatures to the best possible acts and values which are possible at each moment in creaturely existence.

Part Three, accordingly, will argue that much of the world's evil can be explained as the unavoidable consequence of creaturely free will. This free will, however, is not to be seen as a gift from God whereby he has voluntarily limited his power by giving us a share of his creativity; it is, rather, an ontological necessity that creatures have some independence and autonomy--to varying degrees, of course, depending upon their level of mental development. Otherwise, they would not be "creatures." Evil is largely attributed to the misuse of this creaturely freedom, since the power we have for causing goods is also the power for causing evils. And, indeed, the more freedom we creatures have, the greater are the opportunities for immense moral goods and also for more ghastly evils.

Evil is understood by process thought, furthermore, as necessarily built into the world as the by-product of natural laws. As Whitehead explains, "the categories governing the determination of things are the reasons why there should be evil."[85] God has brought about, from an original chaos and through a long evolutionary process, a world of ever-increasing complexity. With each new level of complexity which develops, there arises not only new possibilities for higher goods (new levels of intensity and harmony in the experiences of creatures), but also new possibilities for more devastating evil and suffering. God continues to encourage this evolutionary advance, however, for the sake of aesthetic value. Like all other beings, God seeks experiences of significant value, experiences which avoid the triviality of an absolute chaos as well as, at the other extreme, the monotony of an absolute order wherein there would be no discord and, consequently, no significant aesthetic value either.

A further aspect of process theodicy is its understanding of the "overcoming" of evil. God transforms evil by experiencing it (together with the world's goods) in everlastingly perfect perspective, and he then passes his perfect vision back into the world for its benefit. We shall examine this argument together with the closely related question of human immortality, noting in particular the position of the majority of process thinkers that the only immortality human beings are likely to experience is an "objective" immortality, that is, as memories in God's eternal mind. Process thinkers argue that "personal" or "subjective" immortality is unrealistic, problematic and in fact nonessential either for solving the theodicy issue or for guaranteeing the ultimate value and meaning of our lives.

Before turning to a detailed discussion of these themes, however, I wish to consider another—and a most intriguing—aspect of process theodicy, at least as it is

represented in Hartshorne's writings: his contention that
since God's existence is a <u>necessary</u> truth, evil cannot be
cited as decisive evidence against his existence.

Chapter 5: EVIL AND GOD'S NECESSARY EXISTENCE

Despite the fact that "natural theology" has largely been on the wane since the critiques of Hume and Kant (at least outside the Roman Catholic tradition), Hartshorne has insisted that it is possible to demonstrate that there are in fact rational grounds in support of theistic belief.[86] In this chapter, I wish to outline some of his arguments for God's existence as a necessary, a priori truth, and assess their implications for the theodicy issue.

Hartshorne has little patience with the theological type of protest against any attempt to establish rational grounds for religious beliefs.[87] He is aware, of course, that there has been a long and honored tradition throughout Christian history which has focused on the fallen and corrupted state of human reason and which, consequently, has pointed to the reliance upon revelation (personal and biblical) as the only means of gaining knowledge of God. And indeed, he is aware that no one can question the fact that human rationality is limited and inadequate not only in knowing the physical world but even more so in knowing the spiritual realm. Yet Hartshorne insists that it would seem to be unnecessarily stifling to legitimate religious inquiry simply to reject the use of reason altogether. Unquestioning faith in the Bible's revelations or in the intuitions of "religious experience" is not the sole, legitimate criterion for trusting one's religious beliefs. Faith seeks and requires whatever rational support it can find, for while the "pure in heart" may be truly blessed

and in no need of rational support for their faith, yet, as
Hartshorne points out, how many "are so pure that they can
believe even if they are aware that no reasoner thinks that
reasoning favors belief?"[88] The answer, surely, is:
very few! And further, if there were in fact no rational
arguments in support of religious doctrines, however
limited, partial and incomplete this rational support might
be, would not this in itself "be a strong and quite
rational argument against belief?"[89] The role of
theology is to illuminate religious beliefs, to render them
more explicit, more systematic and comprehensible--in
short, to demonstrate their rational viability, as far as
this is possible. And it is, of course, this role which
Hartshorne has undertaken. But what he defends is a
drastically revised conception of God (the process God),
and not the traditional Christian conception which he and
other process thinkers reject as thoroughly invalid and
indefensible. Hartshorne's voluminous writings in large
part seek to formulate and rationally defend a conception
of God which is both philosophically sound and religiously
adequate, a conception, that is, which escapes both the
inner contradictions and inconsistencies of the traditional
theism, and which is a worthy object of religious devotion
and worship.

GOD AS UNSURPASSABLE

Hartshorne contends that the traditional theistic
proofs are inadequate. Yet this is so not because proofs
for God are impossible, but because the traditional proofs
sought to establish a conception of God which was itself
invalid! The conception of God as a "purely absolute,
infinite and eternal reality is riddled with antimonies"
which effectively render any alleged proof for such a God

"equally illogical."[90]   Hume and Kant have long been
credited with devastating the traditional proofs, and yet
what they refuted were in fact "propositions that rational
theology has no need to affirm."[91]   Traditional theism
defined God as absolutely unsurpassable, a God whose
perfection lies in his independence of all others, in his
static completeness.   There can be no potentiality in such
a God, since he is "a reality in which nothing positive is
left merely potential."[92]   But Hartshorne's point is that
the "ens realissimum is not simply undemonstrable . . . .
but it is indeed demonstrably impossible . . . [and] not
what 'God' as a religious term ought to mean."[93]   God's
perfection, according to process thought, lies not in his
immutable unsurpassability, but in the fact that he is
surpassable by nothing, nothing that is, except himself!
His nature is immutable in some respects (for example, in
its perfect love and knowledge of all that is actual and
possible), yet he is also mutable or processive in some
respects, since he responds to and is partially influenced
by the acts and decisions of his creatures.[94]   In this
way, he continually surpasses himself in perfection, always
perfectly responding to every new experience and to each
new act of his creatures:

> Instead of ascribing to the Unsurpassable the
> actualization of all possible perfection, we
> should ascribe to him the actual possession only
> of all in fact actualized values.   The entire
> world is his to enjoy in all-embracing vision.
> We should further ascribe to him the potential
> possession of every possible value.   Were such
> and such a possible value actual for anyone, it
> would a fortiori be actual for God, who would
> enjoy unsurpassable knowledge of it.   For no mode

of possession of value is more absolute than
full awareness . . . . The divine actuality is
logically coextensive with all actuality and,
in this case, is actuality itself; the divine
potentiality is coextensive with all
possibility and is possibility itself. Any
actual thing God enjoys actually; any possible
thing would be his actual possession were it
actual for anyone. From this 'modal
coincidence' it follows that though God can
increase in value, he can be surpassed by no
other than himself.[95]

God's nature, according to Hartshorne and other process
thinkers, is not solely absolute, immutable, independent,
etc., but rather "dipolar:" God is both immutable and
mutable, both necessary and contingent, both absolute and
relative, and so on--Part Two will provide a more detailed
discussion of this and other aspects of the process
conception of God.

THE TRADITIONAL PROOFS

In proposing to demonstrate that belief in God is
rationally viable, Hartshorne, we must point out, does not
suggest that there are proofs for God which are conclusive
to such a degree that there are no longer grounds for
disagreement. To believe there can be such proofs is a
misunderstanding of what a philosophical proof is: it is
not "a set of undeniable or axiomatic premises from which
the desired conclusion could be deduced,"[96] for if this
were the case, there would hardly be any philosophical
doctrine which could be "proven." The function of a
philosophical proof, rather, "is to establish a price for
rejecting its conclusions,"[97] that is, (in regard to the

theistic proofs) to expose the logical price for rejecting belief in God.[98] The theistic proofs "consist in making explicit what the denial of theism implies,"[99] a denial which Hartshorne believes is counterintuitive and, indeed, "not only unacceptable as true but absurd, not genuinely conceivable."[100] In short, the theistic proofs lead us to assume that if God does not exist, then certain fundamental truths must be denied; "the idea of God, taken as true, is required for the interpretation of some fundamental aspect of life or existence."[101] If belief in God is rejected as absurd, then so likewise (for example) "is the idea of rational ethics, or of a value to human life from the standpoint of the ultimate long view. And then what is not absurd?"[102]

Hartshorne complains that the traditional theistic proofs are unconvincing not only (as we have noted) because they seek to establish a conception of God which is itself invalid, but also, and equally importantly, because they have been formulated rather poorly: "the traditional statements, and traditional evaluations, of the proofs are mostly careless, sloppy, or unfair. In no portion of their responsibility," Hartshorne contends, "have members of my profession done so poorly as in this one."[103] The common view has been that only the ontological proof is an a priori argument (an argument from concepts) while the other proofs are a posteriori arguments (arguments from empirical data).[104] Yet Hartshorne's contention is that all of the proofs must be presented as a priori arguments if they are to have any validity. No empirical argument for God, he insists, can possibly be valid--this was Anselm's "great discovery."[105] The very idea of God as the perfect and unsurpassable being implies that he must exist necessarily or else the concept "God" is incoherent. His existence cannot be contingent. It cannot be dependent upon contingent factors and it "could not possibly be disconfirmed by a contingent fact."[106] In short, there is simply no possibility "to observe some positive fact incompatible with . . . [God's] existence" since the very "definition of God excludes this possibility; a fact incompatible with his existence would mean that, were he to exist, he would owe his existence to the nonbeing of the supposed fact."[107] Proofs for God, accordingly, which argue from contingent facts are wrongly conceived and invalid. This is demonstrated, for example, by the traditional version of the design argument which assumes that God can exist only if a certain order prevails; this wrongly implies that God's existence could be falsified by the negative evidence that the required conditions were absent.[108] The argument (see below) must be formulated in a priori terms; it must demonstrate that any world requires God. "All the proofs," Hartshorne insists, "properly stated, proceed from ideas; but not all from the idea of God itself [as in the ontological proof]. And all show that we must either admit some basic idea to be absurd, or take it to be necessarily true, and admit that this truth entails the necessary existence of the Greatest being."[109]

HARTSHORNE'S PROOFS FOR GOD'S EXISTENCE

Hartshorne has formulated no less than six theistic proofs, all of which, as he points out, "are phases of one 'global' argument, that the properly formulated theistically religious view of life and reality is the most intelligible, self-consistent, and satisfactory one that can be conceived."[110] Besides his extremely important and influential work in reopening serious discussion on the ontological proof, Hartshorne has versions of the aesthetic, ethical, epistemological, teleological and cosmological proofs. All are a priori in that rather than arguing from empirical evidence to God, they argue from concepts. The proofs, in other words, are purely conceptual attempts at linguistic clarification: "Grubbing among facts is neither here nor there. Self-understanding is the issue: someone is confused, either the theist, or the nontheist."[111] It is, Hartshorne suggests, a "logical scandal" that for centuries it was common practice to believe that God is wholly necessary and yet that our evidence of him must be wholly empirical![112]

It would seem appropriate at this point to look briefly at two or three of Hartshorne's proofs. His formulation of the teleological argument (the argument from design), for example, can be simply put: "the world is orderly, order implies an orderer, [and] the only conceivable orderer for a world is God."[113] To deny the conclusion, that God must exist, is to deny one or more of the premises. Hartshorne admits, of course, that many would be all-too-willing to deny the premises, for it seems highly unlikely that "premises acceptable to everyone from which theism can validly be deduced" can ever be formulated.[114] Hartshorne, however, believes that the proper formulation of the proofs will at least show how high a price must be paid for the rejection of their premises, a rejection which he feels is "much more clearly counterintuitive than the simple rejection" of belief in God.[115] He concedes that while "it is unrealistic to hope that all doubts concerning theism can be removed by deductive argument," yet "it may be quite as unrealistic to suppose that no doubts can be removed."[116] The price of rejecting the proofs may appear to some people to be "far higher than they first suspected" and indeed, for some,

"unbearably high."[117] Is one willing to deny, for
example, the first premise of the teleological proof, that
the world is orderly? Surely an "unordered world is a
contradiction in terms" for "it is no object of possible
knowledge and there is no way to distinguish it clearly
from nothing at all."[118] And what of the second
premise? Is one willing to deny that the order which
exists among individuals means that some unitary influence
or power must be acting upon those individuals?; or the
third premise, that only a "power superior in principle to
ordinary powers, only divine power, could constitute the
cosmic orderer?"[119] This is not to say, however, that
one power (God) has a monopoly of power (the literal
meaning of "omnipotence") and that, accordingly, he
controls the world's creatures as he alone sees fit.
Hartshorne and other process thinkers insist that such a
conception of divine power is a pseudoconcept which, if
true, would deny the reality of freely creative creatures.
If God were literally all-powerful, there could be nothing
over which he has power, for all creatures would be
powerless and, as such, would be no more than merely
attributes of God. The argument in favor of the proof's
premises is that the world's order would be impossible if
the world's free agents were not somehow influenced (though
not coercively) by a supreme agent. A multitude of agents
could not form even a disorderly world.[120] That God
persuasively orders the world's freely creative acts in
such a way which permits a significant degree of creaturely
freedom, furthermore, effectively explains why the world is
not a perfect harmony, why it is not a conflict-free
utopia:

> if there is a multiplicity of powers . . . then
> the total cosmic effort cannot be determined by

the supreme power alone. Even the supreme
power can only impose limits on the
disagreements, conflicts, or confusions among
lesser powers; it cannot simply eliminate these
confusions, for this would require it becoming
the sole power, and this is nonsense. Power
acts upon power, not upon the powerless.[121]

The world order, in sum, requires God as its orderer,
"because apart from God there is no way to understand how
there could be any limits at all to the confusion and
anarchy implied by the notion of a multiplicity of creative
agents, none universally influential or wise."[122]

Some will object, to be sure, that there can be an
order without an orderer, that the order is due, for
example, simply to impersonal "laws of nature." But
Hartshorne would counter this with the argument that such
laws are the very question at issue, not the explanation.
It is, he believes, far less problematic to believe in God
as the cosmic orderer than to believe "that a multitude of
individuals, by blind chance, necessity, or deliberate
intention, cooperated to produce or maintain a world
order."[123]

Hartshorne follows a similar logic in regard to the
moral (or ethical) proof. Kant, he suggests, was right in
so far as he saw that a rational ethics requires the summum
bonum; yet Kant misconceived the proper content of this
supreme rational aim by insisting that it is we creatures
(that, human beings) who in some post-terrestrial domain
will enjoy the "supreme good" of virtue and
happiness.[124] Hartshorne argues, to the contrary, that
it is God, not human beings, who enjoys this highest good.
Yet every creaturely act and thought has ultimate meaning
and value in the very fact that it is eternally part of

God's experience. "Rationality as such requires that there
be an aim which it is rational to pursue in spite of the
mortality of nondivine individuals and species of
individuals. But only deity provides a clear meaning for
immortality."[125] Without God, our acts would have no
present or lasting meaning. The price, accordingly, of
denying God's existence is the denial of the meaningfulness
of our acts and the distinction between right and wrong,
good and bad. Without God, the ultimate meaning and value
of our lives must be attributed to one of the following
alternatives, all of which Hartshorne finds absurd: the
short-run consequences of our acts gives them meaning; the
long-run consequences of our acts for the human race gives
them meaning; or the long-run consequences of our acts for
individuals conceived as surviving death forever gives our
acts meaning.[126] But the first proposal seems "to
destroy any genuine rationality in ethics" for it denies
the very possibility of an ultimate value and meaning to
our lives.[127] The second proposal, which Hartshorne
refers to as "social immortality," is, unfortunately,
"wholly indeterminate for human knowledge"[128] and in fact
appears to many as unintelligible: "[s]ince both
individuals and species are mortal . . . . the long-run
prospect is of the total fading out of any good
achieved."[129] And as for the third proposal, the belief
in "personal immortality," the "obvious objection,"
according to Hartshorne, is "that we not only do not know
our individual immortality, but there are a priori
arguments against it. Immortality is a divine trait, why
should it be ours? We are limited spatially, why not
temporally?"[130] In a later chapter we shall discuss in
more detail Hartshorne's arguments against both social and
personal immortality, and examine his alternative theory

(derived from Whitehead and shared by most process
thinkers) of "objective immortality." For the present,
however, I wish to draw attention to Hartshorne's point
that "a part of the price of nonbelief" is "that there can
be no positive rational aim, intelligible as such . . . . .
For the unbeliever there can be only a vague hope that
somehow something good, we know not what, will in the long
run ensue from our efforts."[131] With belief in God,
however, there is a rational aim and, accordingly, an
ultimate meaning for our lives. All that we have
experienced contributes to God's eternal experience and is
remembered fully and perfectly forever. This is true
worship and service of God, to contribute to his
experience--rather than egoistically expecting that we
ourselves must live forever, consciously, if our acts are
to have ultimate, and hence present, meaning.

We turn now to Hartshorne's important writings on
the ontological proof. He was among the first to uncover
and exploit a "second" ontological argument for God's
existence in Anselm's writings, an argument which had
generally been unnoticed by critics and defenders of the
proof alike.[132] Hartshorne contends that the second
argument, found in Proslogion, Chapter III, is immune to
the traditional criticisms of the proof, and that by
utilizing a proper conception of God (Anselm's conception
was incoherent) the proof can be defended as a rationally
valid argument. The first version, found in Proslogion,
Chapter II, may be formulated, in brief, as follows:
"Existence is good, hence the best conceivable thing [that
is, God] must have it, and hence must exist."[133] Yet
Kant, and before him Gassendi, rightly objected that
"existence is not a property which a thing may have or
lack, for without existence there is nothing to have or to

lack properties." Hartshorne agrees: "An idea or definition attributes properties hypothetically, it says what a thing of a certain sort must be like if there exists such a thing. Hence, existence is not one of the properties in question."[134] Yet the second argument is quite distinct, "independent" and "logically irreducible" to the first. In the second argument, Anselm proposed that "[t]o exist necessarily is better than to exist contingently; hence the greatest conceivable being can exist only necessarily. Moreover, whatever could be necessary is necessary ("reduction principle" of modal logic)."[135] Hartshorne points out, accordingly, that Anselm understood, where countless others have not, that God must exist necessarily or not at all. God, as the unsurpassable being (the definition of God Hartshorne accepts and which is implied in Anselm's phrase, "that than which nothing greater can be conceived")[136] must exist necessarily, for contingency implies weakness and imperfection--an argument Hartshorne refers to as "Anselm's Principle."[137] Anselm showed that "to exist contingently, or so that non-existence would have been possible, is to exist as other than divine. Only that which could not conceivably fail to exist can be unsurpassable or worthy of worship, and only that which is unsurpassable could not conceivably fail to exist."[138] It is, therefore, invalid to hold, as many have, that "God's existence is necessary only upon condition that He exist."[139] For, "[w]ere God to exist, yet his nonexistence to be conceivable, he would either exist by sheer chance or luck, or else owing to some cause. Either way," as Hartshorne insists, "he would not be the best conceivable being, and hence would not be worthy of worship as God."[140] If the concept of God is conceivable as a consistent idea, then God must exist necessarily.

Yet, of course, "positivists" (that is, those who regard as meaningless questions of metaphysics and theology) contend that the concept of God is not coherently conceivable, that the idea of God cannot be shown to have consistent cognitive meaning.[141] Hartshorne concedes that this contention attacks the ontological proof (and all of the other proofs which he has formulated as arguments which are equally a priori) at their "weakest," "most vulnerable point."[142] He points out, furthermore, that the conception of God which supposedly was to be proved by the traditional versions of the proofs is indeed incoherent. Anselm, for example, spoiled his important discovery with an understanding of God as absolutely independent and immutable, and as unsurpassable in the sense that he was conceived as the sum of all actuality, all perfections and hence statically complete. Anselm's "major mistake was that he failed to explore the possible ways of defining perfection, and for this and other reasons failed to realize that his own definition was incoherent and not an 'idea' in the required sense."[143] "Anselm's own idea of God was in truth absurd, so that for this idea positivism is actually valid."[144]

The understanding of the divine unsurpassability as a static fullness is invalid, according to process thinkers, for a number of reasons. For one thing, there simply can be no complete actualization of all possibilities, for not all possibilities are compatible. The idea of God as statically complete, as the absolute maximization of all possibilities, furthermore, is no more coherent than "a greatest number" or a "greatest possible value."[145] As statically complete, God would render invalid the essential contrast between actuality and

possibility (for there would be no potentiality left to
actualize) and this would hopelessly compromise our
struggle to realize possible values.[146] Hartshorne's
proposal, as we have noted previously, is that a more
defensible understanding of God's unsurpassable perfection
is that he is unsurpassable except by himself. His
knowledge, for example, is perfect, and yet as creatures
continually actualize new possibilities (making determinate
what was previously merely an indeterminate potentiality),
God's experiences of these actualized values add to the
content of his knowledge.[147] God cannot be the static
maximization of all there is to know since there are
continually new things to know. He knows the actual only
as actual and the possible only as possible. And, of
course, while God is continually self-surpassing in his
knowledge of new actualities, this does not imply that he
changes into a more perfect being, into something other
than he was; what occurs rather is that he continually
changes into "a more excellent state of the same
being."[148]

     Hartshorne argues that while the classical idea of
God is rightly rejected by positivists as incoherent, the
process God does not suffer from this defect. It is, he
feels, simply incredulous to deny that the idea of God, as
process thinkers have formulated it, has cognitive import
when the very idea--and it alone--explicates "the meaning
of cosmic order, the meaning of a rational aim in
ethics,"[149] and so on, as Hartshorne has shown in his
versions of the theistic proofs. If God did not exist,
then some fundamental truths about reality would have to be
denied, a denial which is both absurd and
counterintuitive. He argues, furthermore, that God's
existence is one of several "metaphysical truths" which, as

a priori necessities, cannot be falsified.[150] The burden
of proof, Hartshorne insists, is on the positivists, not on
the theists, for "what can it mean to say that a doctrine,
against which there can be no evidence, yet might be
false?"[151]

But let us turn to a related point, one which is of
central importance to Hartshorne's attempt to validate the
theistic proofs. Anselm's insight that God must
necessarily exist is, he believes, correct, and yet he is
quick to point out that this does not mean that everything
about God is necessary.[152] It is one thing to exist
necessarily, yet another, for example, to know
necessarily. If God's knowledge of the world were a
necessary knowledge, then (despite Aquinas) the content of
his knowledge would likewise be necessary. But, of course,
this would effectively deny the contingency and freedom of
creaturely acts, a denial which is absurd. The process
thinkers' radically revised understanding of God, as noted
previously (see also Chapter 6), is that he is to be
defined as "dipolar:" he exists necessarily, yet he has
contingent aspects, or as Hartshorne puts it, contingent
actuality. God knows the actual world fully and perfectly,
but the content of his knowing is contingent since that
which he experiences is continually processing, continually
changing as creatures actualize ever-new values. It is
this distinction between God's necessary existence and his
contingent actuality which Hartshorne believes permits him
to escape the criticism of the traditional ontological
proof that it invalidly derives God's concrete actuality
from a mere definition.[153] Hartshorne agrees with the
accepted and apparently unanimous consensus of opinion that
we cannot deduce the concrete from an abstract definition
(that is, we cannot establish God's concrete reality by

logical means); yet he denies that the ontological proof, properly formulated, makes this move. Hartshorne insists, to be sure, that God's necessary existence must be actualized in some concrete state, but the proof deduces only God's bare existence as a necessary truth; how it is actualized cannot be deduced by a priori argument (since God's actualized states are contingent).[154] The ontological argument shows, nevertheless, that God's existence is either necessarily exemplified or his existence is absurd. God cannot be "contingently exemplified" or "contingently unexemplified," for if his existence was not necessarily exemplified in concrete states, he would be less than unsurpassable.[155] If nonexemplification were even possible, God would, in fact, be surpassable, and he would then be contingently existent and not God at all.

IMPLICATIONS FOR THEODICY

The issue which concerns us in this chapter is, however, not to assess the validity of Hartshorne's theistic proofs--this would be an enormous and complex task. And while I believe he is correct in his central assumption that the proofs are to be formulated as a priori arguments, and that the essential point is to see that "God" is either a conceivable idea or absurd, implying that he either exists necessarily or not at all, my present intention is to focus solely upon the implications of Hartshorne's proofs for the theodicy issue. The main implication can be readily stated: if God's existence can, in fact, be established as an a priori necessity, then evil (or any other contingent fact) cannot count as decisive evidence against his existence. In this Hartshorne seems correct and, as he points out, even Hume admitted this:

"[t]he argument from evil makes the assumption that theism
is not an a priori or necessary truth. It is to the great
credit of David Hume that he saw this and . . . admitted
explicitly that were there reason to classify theism as a
priori, then counter arguments from evil would not be
relevant.   No   empirical   evidence   can   negate   a
necessity."[156]   Hartshorne   concludes,   accordingly,   that
"the 'problem of evil' is a mistake, a pseudoproblem."[157]
It is, he argues, simply not valid to ask whether evil can
be   reconciled   with   God's   very   existence,   for   God's
existence is a necessary truth which no contingent fact (of
which evil is the most pressing instance) can deny.

    This being the case, discussion of the theodicy
issue, it would appear, could well end here. Yet it does
not, and for good reasons! There do not appear to be many
philosophers and theologians, especially outside the Roman
Catholic tradition, who share Hartshorne's belief in the
viability of rational proofs for God, despite his efforts
to convince them otherwise. Any theodicy, accordingly, (or
any theism) based upon the assumed validity of the proofs
would be unacceptable. What is required is to demonstrate
that the conception of God assumed by the proofs and
utilized in reference to the theodicy issue is coherent,
and as we have noted, Hartshorne has several arguments in
support of this contention. One argument, however, which
we have not yet mentioned is perhaps the most relevant to
the theodicy issue.   In short, Hartshorne seeks to
demonstrate the coherence of his conception of God by
showing that it is, in fact, reconcilable with the
empirical fact of evil. He realizes that God's necessary
existence can be established by the theistic proofs only if
the conception of God employed in the proofs is coherently

conceivable, and perhaps the most forceful way to
demonstrate this coherence is to show that the process God
is reconcilable with evil. This is not to say that unless
God is shown to be reconcilable with evil he does not
exist, for the very essence of Hartshorne's a priori logic
is that God's necessary existence is established without
reference to empirical facts. Yet to deal more forcefully
with the positivists' objection (and with those who, for
whatever reason, cannot accept the validity of theistic
proofs), Hartshorne seeks to show that God's concrete
actuality is reconcilable with evil. God's bare existence
is expressed concretely by his power and goodness (and in
other ways), and if these aspects of God can be shown to be
reconcilable with evil, this would seem not only to go a
long way toward establishing the validity of the conception
of God employed in Hartshorne's versions of the proofs,
but, I would suggest, it would also represent in itself a
possible solution to the theodicy question without
reference to the proofs!

I would suggest, furthermore, that this latter
approach to the theodicy issue is far more useful and
potentially acceptable than the former, for even if God's
existence were established beyond doubt (were this
possible) as an a priori necessity, this tells us only that
evil does not count against God's existence, but it does
not tell us anything about why God permits (or causes) the
evil! Griffin has put this rather well: "simply showing
the bare possibility that God's existence might not be
contradicted by the world's evil does not," he contends,
"do much toward solving the problem of evil." What is
needed is "a 'global argument,' the purpose of which is to
show that a theistic interpretation can illuminate the
totality of our experience, including the experience of

evil, better than nontheistic interpretations."[158] A successful solution to the theodicy issue must show how evil is reconcilable with God, with his power and goodness. Hartshorne, of course, does realize this, that a viable solution to the theodicy issue requires more than the theistic proofs. He has pointed out that his contribution to theodicy has been to employ not only "the logic of contingency and necessity," but also the "use of [Whitehead's doctrine of] creative freedom."[159] While the former refers to his a priori theistic proofs (and the formulation of metaphysical "first principles"), the latter refers to his attempt to define the range and extent of creaturely freedom and moral responsibility for good and evil acts, and correspondingly, an understanding of God which is consistent with such. The remainder of this book will examine this aspect of Hartshorne's theodicy, a theodicy which, as noted in Chapter 4, is centred upon his revised conception of God, upon a revised free will defence, upon certain aesthetic considerations, and upon arguments about how evil is "overcome" by God. I believe this theodicy is an important and illuminating contribution to the current discussion, and I most heartily agree with John Cobb that "Hartshorne's greatest achievement is not his brilliant revival of certain arguments for the existence of God but his development of a concept of God fully compatible with all we know about the world, self-consistent with itself and of profound religious significance."[160]

PART TWO: THE PROCESS GOD

Process thinkers reject the conception of God which has dominated much of Christian theological reflection. "Traditional" or "classical" Christianity defines God as a wholly necessary, totally independent, immutable, all-powerful Being, "the sum of all possible perfections--the actuality, without remainder, of all possible real value."[1] According to process thinkers, however, such a conception of God makes it impossible to defend the essential theological beliefs that God loves his creatures, that he is affected by their acts and decisions, and, indeed, that creatures have genuine freedom vis-à-vis the divine causal agency. Creaturely acts and decisions cannot affect the immutable God of traditional Christianity, other than by the fact that he has created this world rather than another (or none at all). Neither can there be acts and decisions of creatures which, in any genuine sense, can be described as free, since God knows all things eternally, immutably, and necessarily.

In this second part, I wish to present the alternative conception of God which has been developed by process thinkers, most notably by Charles Hartshorne. I shall focus in particular upon his reinterpretations of the centrally important divine attributes of immutability and omnipotence. The process God is conceived, as we shall see, as dipolar, dynamic, socially interrelated and a persuasive causal agency in the world. The implications of this understanding of God for the theodicy issue will be discussed in Part Three, but first a number of critical issues must be addressed in this present section.

Chapter 6:   GOD AS PROCESSIVE

Traditional Christian theology has insisted that God is wholly immutable and independent. God cannot change or be affected by his creatures, since, it is held, any change would imply that he would either acquire some perfection (and hence was not perfect before acquiring it) or that he would lose some perfection (and hence would no longer be perfect). Process thinkers, however, protest that this understanding of God is inconsistent not only with Jesus' revelation of a God that is intimately related to us, but also with our continuing religious sensibilities of a responsive, loving God. Hartshorne insists that a

> deity who cannot in any sense change or have contingent properties is a being for whom whatever happens in the contingent world is literally a matter of indifference. Such a being is totally "impassible" toward all things, utterly insensitive and unresponsive. This is the exact denial that "God is love." It means that nothing we can possibly do, enjoy, or suffer can in any way whatever contribute a satisfaction or value to the divine life greater or different from what this life would have possessed had we never existed or had our fortunes been radically other than they are. Strange that for so many centuries it was held legitimate to call such a deity a God of love, or purpose, or knowledge!

What we really have is the idea of sheer power,
sheer causation, by something wholly neutral as to
what, if anything, may be its effects.[2]

For God's interrelationship with the world to be
conceptualized more adequately, process thinkers insist
that we must acknowledge there is a real and mutual
interdependence between God and the world. This, of
course, does not imply that the relationship is between
equals: God remains the supreme power, yet not the only
power. That, furthermore, this apparent limitation of
divine omnipotence does not negate God's absolute
perfection is insisted upon by process thinkers. God
remains the greatest conceivable being, yet his perfection
is understood not as a purely static, immutable essence,
but in his ability to respond to all contingencies in
perfect love, justice, knowledge and power. It is
erroneous to conceive of divine love as nothing but giving,
for love (as human experience understands it) involves not
only giving to another, but being responsive to the other.
"A new era in religion," Hartshorne believes, "may be
predicted as soon as men grasp the idea that it is just as
true that God is the supreme beneficiary or recipient of
achievement . . . as that he is the supreme benefactor or
source of achievement."[3]

ACTUAL ENTITIES AND PERSONS

To more fully appreciate the process thinkers'
conception of God, it is necessary to be aware of certain
fundamental aspects of process metaphysics. In close
affinity with modern physics, process thinkers define the
world as constituted not by a dualism of matter and souls,
or by "things" in empty space, or by essentially static
substances, but rather by "quantum units" of energy, called

"actual entities" by Whitehead. These entities are the "ultimate reals" of which the world is constituted; they are microscopic and momentary "drops of experience,"[4] various groupings of which constitute the manifold objects of our empirical senses--human beings, trees, animals, etc. Actual entities, however, are not merely microscopic, simple, or of temporally short duration. The two paradigm cases of actual entities suggested by Whitehead are that of subatomic particles, to be sure, but also each momentary experience of a human being: the myriad of actual entities which constitute a human being are themselves unified by a central group of entities (the brain), such that each unified experience is itself the act of an actual entity.[5] All actual entities causally influence other actual entities, furthermore, such that each internally affects countless others. An individual actual entity is a synthesis, a "becoming," a "concrescence" of other actual entities which are the data of its experience.

That all life is not merely a chaotic and random flux of entities is ensured by the fact that continuity of character and "personal identity" are accounted for in so far as certain mental and physical patterns repeat themselves in the processive sequences which constitute all creatures.[6] Human beings, for example, are composed of many "societies" of actual entities, controlled and unified by a central "regnant nexus," the brain. As such, and like all other creatures, human beings are "dipolar," for besides our ever-changing, ever-processing reality at each moment, there remains a more constant "essence" or "being" which gives functional unity to the entities that constitute our sequences of experience. This "essence" is not an independent or static substance,[7] but rather those mental and physical patterns of actual entities which are repeated in sequence.

Hartshorne has appealed to Morris Cohen's "law of polarity" to support the thesis that all things are necessarily dipolar: "ultimate contraries are correlatives, mutually interdependent, so that nothing real can be described by the wholly one-sided assertion of simplicity, being, actuality, and the like, each in a 'pure' form, devoid and independent of [its polar opposite:] complexity, becoming, potentiality, and related contraries."[8] Human beings are dipolar to the extent that we are both the cause of some acts and affected by others; we are both concretely actual and yet have future potential; we are both simple (as unified centers of consciousness) and complex (as a processive sequence of myriads of actual entities). Human beings are dipolar also in the sense that the actual entities which constitute us have both "physical poles" (which largely repeat past physical data) and "mental poles" (which appropriate novel possibilities).

All reality is a "social process" of interrelated, interdependent, processing creatures composed of actual entities. All creatures are engaged in a "creative advance" toward novelty--a perpetual, incessant quest for intensity of experience and for aesthetic harmony and value. In this quest, every entity has "intrinsic reference . . . to preceding occasions with which it has some degree of sympathetic participation, echoing their qualities, but with an overall quality of its own as it reacts to them."[9] Our most fundamental experience reveals that the essence of life is to be related, not to be immutable or independent. "Whatever else the self is, it is hardly a substance which, in Descartes' phrase, 'requires nothing but itself in order to exist,' . . . .

To the contrary, the very being of the self is relational
or social; and it is nothing if not a process of change
involving the distinct modes of present, past, and
future."[10]

PROCESS THEISM AND TRADITIONAL THEISM

This understanding of the dipolar, processive and
socially interdependent nature of reality has, for process
thinkers, immense implications for conceptualizing God.
Rather than conceiving God as a static, unrelated,
immutable Being, process thinkers define him as dipolar,
processive, and socially related to his creatures. God is
understood as the "chief exemplification" of the
metaphysical categories which define all life, rather than
their exception.[11] God is both immutable in his essence,
and yet mutable in his response to creaturely acts and
decisions; he is the supreme cause of all things, yet he is
also affected by the acts and decisions of his creatures;
his being is immutable, yet his becoming is the expression
of that being at each processive moment; he is infinite in
his awareness of all potentiality, yet finite in his
knowledge of the world's actualities (for these are
finite); he is necessary in his a priori existence and
steadfast character, yet contingent in his response to the
contingencies of the world, for these contingent acts of
his creatures become part of his internal experience.[12]

Process thinkers complain that in traditional
Christian theism, God alone "is asserted to be an absolute
exception to the Law of Polarity."[13] God is defined as
"monopolar;" he is pure being, devoid of becoming; purely
immutable, without process; purely absolute, without
relative aspects; purely necessary, devoid of contingency;
and purely cause, without being affected or influenced by

others. Traditional Christian theism seeks, in effect, to
protect God's absolute perfection by denying that any of
the supposedly inferior and unworthy qualities apply to his
reality. But the question process thinkers raise is
whether this conception of God does not, in fact, render
him religiously inadequate. Is it not inconsistent to
claim that "God is love" and yet define him as wholly
independent and unaffected by the world? Did not Jesus
reveal a responsive, loving, dynamic and related God?
Process thinkers, in sum, reject the monopolar prejudice of
traditional theism, and insist that "experience does not
. . . exhibit the implied essential inferiority of the
theologically despised contraries" (except those that are
themselves genuinely negative, like 'ignorant' and
'involuntary'!)"[14]

Traditional Christian theism, to be sure, does seek
to reconcile its immutable God with the revelation of Jesus
as lovingly involved with the world. The doctrine of the
Incarnation is an important instance of this. Yet
Hartshorne contends that this doctrine, as traditionally
conceived, amounts to an incoherent habit of "simply adding
Jesus to an unreconstructed idea of a non-loving God;"[15]
that is, merely juxtaposing the perfect, tender love of
Jesus to the idea of a self-sufficient and wholly absolute
God. Hartshorne draws the same conclusion with regard to
the traditional doctrine of the Trinity, for it likewise
leaves the reconciliation unresolved:

The Trinity is supposed to meet the requirements
of giving God an object of love which yet agrees
with his absolute self-sufficiency, and also an
object of love "worthy" to be loved with so
perfect a love as the divine. This is done by
making the lover and the beloved identical--yet

not identical. But whatever be the truth of this
idea--whose meaning seems to me just as
problematic as its truth, for once more, nonsense
is only nonsense, however you put a halo around
it--it leaves the essential problem of divine
love unsolved. For either God loves the
creatures or he does not. If he does, then their
interests contribute to his interests, for love
means nothing more than this. If he does not,
then the essence of religious belief in God is
sacrificed, and one still has the question, How
then is God related to the creatures'
interests?[16]

Traditional Christian theism would appear to be
suffering from an overdose of Greek metaphysics, a
Hellenization of the Gospels which results in an unstable
compound that weakens its religious force and philosophical
viability. Indeed:

Is it not . . . the case, that the conviction
that God is [solely] immutable is part of the
Hellenistic rather than the biblical heritage?
And, while it was taken up into Christianity by
Scholasticism, is it not a fair question to ask
whether this aspect of the Hellenization of the
Gospels did not itself violate the biblical
vision of the personal God . . . . and what sense
can we make of a person, either human or divine,
who is so unrelated as to be unaffected by
others?[17]

Traditional theism makes God the one exception to
our common understanding of the social nature of reality,
for whereas to "know" or "love" something is understood to
imply that we are internally affected by it, God's knowing

and loving are said to be just the opposite. Aquinas informed us that God's relationship with the world "is not real in God objectively, but is only attributed to Him by extrinsic denomination because of the way minds have to think about Him as cause."[18] The relationship, in short, is only in our minds; it is a relation of reason ("relatio rationis") which does not affect God's immutable essence, for "God is already and from all eternity positively infinite in the fullness of his perfection."[19] Aquinas' position implies that "God, unlike creatures, must in his knowing in no way depend upon or be conditioned by what He knows. God, accordingly, does not know creatures because they are present to Him in their finite existence; rather, they exist because he knows them [eternally]." In short, "what Thomas seems to offer me is the assurance that God does not know the contingent 'me' in my factual existence, but only 'me' as a possibility which He has [from eternity] decreed should be fulfilled."[20]

In light of such logic, process thinkers conclude that for Thomists to continue to use the words "know" and "love" in reference to God is not merely analogical (as Thomists admit) but an analogy whose inverted terms are a "blatant equivocation."[21] For not only does their conception of God deny to God any "real" knowledge or love of the world's contingencies, but it also would appear to eliminate all contingency from the world, since God's immutable and eternal knowledge of all creation is a necessary knowledge. It is, in sum, inconsistent to argue that God is absolute and necessary in every respect, and yet that the world he knows is contingent. Aquinas may have believed that God can necessarily know a contingent world, but process thinkers denounce such a position as inconsistent and "beyond intelligible account."[22] It is, furthermore, equally inconsistent to argue, as Thomists do, that God's knowing is beyond past, present, and future modalities. Such a position annihilates the meaning of "now" and the reality of the temporal process.[23]

CONTEMPORARY THOMISTIC THINKING

We might mention here that a growing number of contemporary theologians outside the process school of thought are, like process thinkers, finding the traditional Christian conception of God inadequate. It is significant that many Roman Catholic theologians are among this number (for it is the Thomist God which has been 'the main representative of classical theism attacked by process thinkers).[24] The contemporary Catholic theologian Norris Clarke, S.J., for example, has clearly acknowledged his movement beyond traditional theism:

> In the past Thomistic metaphysicians seem to have been content for the most part to assert and defend the absolute immutability of God and to relegate all change and diversity on the side of the creature. But they have not gone on to explain how He can enter into a truly interpersonal dialogue with created persons, how His loving of them and their response to Him in the particular contingent ways which are proper to a free exchange between persons can truly make a difference to Him, how He is not the completely impassive, indifferent, metaphysical iceberg, or at least one-way, unreceptive Giver, to whom my loving or not loving, my salvation or damnation, make no difference whatever, as Hartshorne and other process philosophers have accused Him of being. It does seem to me that they have a

legitimate grievance against the way Thomists
have handled, or failed to handle, this
problem.[25]

Other contemporary Catholic theologians concur.
James Felt, S.J., for example, admits that it "is time to
revise our traditional metaphysics," since "it is
impossible to reconcile necessary conclusions of Thomas'
system [that God is immutable] with known facts of
experience [that God loves us and responds to us]."[26] The
traditional Thomist formulation of the doctrine of divine
immutability implies that "it must literally be all the
same to God" whether "we rejoice or sorrow, are saved or
are damned."[27] Felt notes that no human love can be
"indifferent to a return of that love;" yet we "find
ourselves forced by our traditional metaphysics to say that
God is--let us admit it--indifferent to our return of love;
otherwise our love, which only we can give, would be of
some value to God! It is not our insights that are at
fault here," Felt concludes, "but our inherited notions
about God's perfection."[28]

Joseph Donceel, S.J., likewise has admitted that "it
is becoming more and more difficult for us to accept"[29]
the implications of the traditional doctrine of divine
immutability; the Thomist "doctrine of the nonreciprocity
of relations needs a thorough reexamination:"[30]

some of the traditional teachings about God seem
to contradict what we know about him from
revelation, what we feel about him in our heart.
The God for whom it makes no difference
whatsoever whether there is a Creation or
Incarnation, the God who is totally unaffected by
human suffering, does not look like the God of
our faith. The God who, by becoming man, is not

different at all from what he would have been if
he had not become man, does not look like the God
of the Bible.[31]

Piet Schoonenberg, S.J., also insists that "we have
to learn from process philosophy . . . that our image of
God must be dipolar,"[32] and, more specifically, that
God's knowing the world implies a real change in God:

How can an action proceed from a being without
becoming also a reality, an act of that being
itself? That is why God's outward activity looks
to us like a real reality in God himself. It
does not seem true either that the efficient
cause as cause has no real, but only a logical
relation to the effect . . . . We admit a real
relation not only from effect to cause, but also
from cause to effect, respectively a passive and
an active relation. That is why we would like to
call real not only the relation from creature to
God but also the relation from God to creature
. . . . God is not "relative" as opposed to
"absolute." But he is "relational," "involved,"
or better still, "involving himself." In this
way he really changes in his perfect outward
activity and relation, without, however, any
imperfection or dependence.[33]

Walter Stokes, S.J., concurs that "the [traditional]
notion that God is an immutable, infinitely perfect Being
is a metaphysical scandal;"[34] and William Hill, O.P.,
suggests that our concept of God "must embrace contingency
and temporality, qualities heretofore understood as
precisely non-divine."[35] He notes that while Whitehead's
dipolar theism is "[a]t the very forefront of all
contemporary efforts to come to grips with the problem,"

Catholic thinking on the issue has been at best "clearly programmatic in kind, tentative probings toward solutions rather than definitive statements, leaving the question an open one."[36]   John Wright, S.J., is also aware that the traditional "God of immutable essence . . . may well be able to exercise absolute initiative, but it is inconceivable how he would respond to a free human response."[37]   Wright concedes that despite the traditional conception, "God the Creator is different from what he would have been had He chosen not to create."[38] Anthony Kelly, C.SS.R., furthermore, admits that traditional theology "has left the reality of God too 'abstract,' not sufficiently involved as an actual, free Presence in human affairs."[39]   "The traditional idea of God as Pure Act, static, impassive, immutable, must be supplanted by an idea of the Divine Reality that is more viable for the modern mind . . . . A purely external relation of reason cannot be sufficient; God must be related to the world with a real internal relatedness."[40] Karl Rahner, S.J., seems to concur also with this basic line of thinking. Rahner distinguishes between God as he is in himself and God as he changes in another: "God can become something, he who is unchanging in himself can himself become subject to change in something else." Indeed, "in and in spite of his immutability, he can truly become something, He himself, he, in time."[41] As one of Rahner's interpreters comments, this position "no longer seems to accept the scholastic doctrine which claims that the only change occurring in the Incarnation happens in the assumed humanity of Christ."[42]

It is clear that these distinguished Catholic theologians have felt pressed to reexamine and further explicate the traditional Thomist understanding of divine

immutability, and many of them have done so in direct
response to the challenge of process thinkers. But these
Thomists do not reject the traditional teachings outright;
they claim, rather, that "latent" and "implicit" aspects of
the writings of Aquinas can be "exploited" in defence of a
reconstructed and more viable Thomism.[43] This attitude
may appear to the outsider to be almost a Thomistic
idolatry; the encouraging point, nevertheless, from the
perspective of process thinkers, is that the work toward
rethinking the traditional doctrine of God is well under
way, and whether Whitehead and Hartshorne are given credit
or credit is given to latent aspects of Thomas' writings is
probably inconsequential. The Thomist proposals, however,
do appear rather rigid and tentative to date, as Hill
acknowledges, and it seems to me that more openness to
process metaphysics and a more cooperative attitude would
be beneficial. Both Thomists and process thinkers regard
themselves as serious interpreters of the one Christian
faith; future theological scholarship, accordingly, surely
could be advanced by a closer dialogue between these two
major schools. They need not remain mutually exclusive,
for, indeed, there would appear to be significant areas
where Thomism can aid process thinking, and vice versa.

An example of the latter can be seen in the response
of Thomists to the process thinkers' insistence that God
must be affected by the world. Many contemporary Thomists
admit this, and yet define this worldly influence upon God
as due to the fact that he has created this particular
world rather than another of an infinite number of possible
worlds. God remains immutable, they hold, since his
intrinsic nature is in no way affected. In a sense this is
quite similar to the proposal of process thinkers: God's
Primordial Nature (his abstract essence) remains immutable

in its love, knowledge, power, etc., while his Consequent
Nature (his sequence of experiences) continually processes
as he appropriates the world's contingencies. These
contingent acts do not add to nor detract from his
immutable Primordial Nature, nor do they alter his perfect
love, knowledge or power. God's experience of the world's
contingent events merely provides a concrete expression of
his immutable qualities. Where process thinkers and
Thomists seem to differ, however, centers about the
question as to whether the contingent acts of creatures are
genuinely new for God, whether they make a difference to
God in this sense.

Norris Clarke proposes an answer from the Thomistic
perspective: rather than enriching God, creaturely acts
are to be seen under the rubric of a logic of
"delimitation:"

> a superior agent freely offers its indeterminate
> abundance of power to a lower agent, allowing the
> latter to channel, or determine--which means here
> to delimit (partially negate)--the flow of the
> former's power along lines determined by the
> lesser agent, to help him execute his own limited
> operation. In this case the determination
> contributed by the lower agent does not add any
> new being to the power of the higher agent. It
> "adds on" only a partial negation or delimitation
> of the higher plenitude, hence does not introduce
> any change in, or addition to, the real being of
> the higher agent.[44]

Lewis Ford's comment on this proposal from the perspective
of process thought is to suggest that Clarke's "logic of
delimitation seems to imply that all these determinations
(including those excluded) are 'already' fully present in

the initial indeterminate abundance of power, and all that
has happened is the singling out of one for its appearance
on the temporal stage of the world."[45] Ford questions, I
think rightly, whether this really permits us to conclude
that our acts are free. Since God "always knows the
creature as part of himself, how can that intentional
content be in any way new?" "[I]t is clear," Ford
contends, "that the contents of God's intentional consciousness are not derived from the external world . . . .
These contingent contents must then derive from God's own
inner being."[46] Acts which seem novel and free to us,
accordingly, are not novel or free from God's ultimate
perspective. It seems to me (as it does to Ford) that
process thought more readily accounts for the freedom,
novelty and the genuine contingency of the world's
creatures. God knows what is possible, indeed probable,
for every situation, but free creatures (however slight
this freedom may be when considered individually) affect
the final determination of events. God's role is not
somehow to predecide all things, but to "lure" creatures to
the best possibilities which are available at each moment.
We shall consider this point later, in more detail.

THE PROCESS GOD

The process thinkers' understanding of God as dipolar,
processive and socially related is based, in large part, on
the assumption that in our everyday understanding, the most
admirable and loving being is he who is the most responsive
to others, not he who is the most independent and
uninfluenced by others. Hartshorne has ably illustrated
this point.[47] Think of a poem, he suggests, that is read
before a glass of water, an ant, a dog, and human beings of
varying degrees of sensitivity. We would expect it to have

virtually no affect on the glass, very little on the ant, more on the dog, and much more on the human beings. We would expect, furthermore, that God, as the most perfect and lovingly responsive Being, would respond to and be affected by the poem most fully. Yet the traditional formulation of divine immutability implies that the poem would have no affect on God at all! What seems, therefore, to be a defect in other beings--the lack of full responsiveness--has been made a perfection in God; God does "less for us than the poorest of human creatures. What we ask above all is the chance to contribute to the being of others."[48] Hartshorne writes:

> "To love," it has been said, "is to wish to give rather than to receive"; but in loving God we are, according to . . . thousands of orthodox divines, forbidden to seek to give; for God, they say, is a totally impassive, nonreceptive, nonrelative being. Such guardians of the divine majesty, in my judgment, know not what they do.[49]

To speak of God as loving us and yet totally independent of and unaffected by our acts and decisions, and by our very existence, seems "nonsense"[50] and, indeed, destroys "the whole point of religion" as the worship and service of God.[51]

Process thinkers, in sum, insist that it is more viable and consistent to think of God not as the sole exception to the processive, dipolar and interrelational nature of reality, but as the chief exemplification of those qualities. God may have an immutable, independent essence--his ethical character and necessary existence--yet he also has a mutable, contingent nature which experiences each new creaturely act and decision, and is internally affected by them. God has not simply caused all things from some first moment in (or before) time, but continually lures and persuades his creatures to actualize the best ideals possible at every moment in the processive sequences of experiences which constitute our realities. Whether or not we creatures do, in fact, actualize these possibilities, God's ever-present, ever-responsive reality takes full account of and values whatever possibilities we decide to actualize, thereby giving them both present and lasting significance.

CRITICAL ISSUES

A number of questions arise from the foregoing discussion. We might ask, for example, whether it is not blatantly anthropomorphic to define God in terms of the categories by which we understand finite reality; does this not undermine the divine uniqueness?; and indeed, is the concept of dipolarity itself not an untenable paradox of juxtapositing polar opposite categories within a single being? Finally, in conceiving God as dipolar, is there not some problem in the implication which arises, that God is necessarily defined in reference to some world, that God needs some world?

To conceptualize God as the eminent exemplification of the metaphysical categories that govern all life is, admittedly, anthropomorphic. Process thinkers, however, do not claim to have literally conceptualized God or to have erased the essential mystery of God, for that mystery will forever remain beyond our full comprehension. What process thinkers claim to have contributed to modern theological studies is an understanding of God which is consistent with our contemporary interpretation of reality. All attempts to conceptualize God have, of course, been anthropomorphic in this sense, for each culture necessarily has conceived God in terms of its own world view. This obviously runs the risk of relativism, for when our world view changes so must our conception of God; yet this risk must be taken if we are to conceptualize God in terms which are relevant and meaningful to contemporary society. The modern world of process, dipolarity and interdependency calls for a conception of God as processive, dipolar and interdependent. This may not be a final or fully literal conceptualization of God, but process thinkers insist that it is at the very least more consistent with our contemporary world view than is the traditional conception of God.

Process thinkers would reject the second criticism (noted above) that to conceive God in terms of the metaphysical categories undermines his uniqueness. That God is the chief or eminent exemplification of the categories is the common teaching of process thinkers, a doctrine which Hartshorne has designated by the principle of "dual transcendence."[52] God exhibits perfectly and, thus, uniquely, the polar categories: he is perfectly immutable (in his constant character) and perfectly mutable (in his response to all contingencies); he is perfectly infinite (in his knowledge of the infinite realm of possibility) and yet perfectly finite (in his response to finite realities); etc.

Against those, furthermore, who would argue that the dipolar conception of God results in an untenable paradox, Hartshorne has pointed out that each being exemplifies the polar opposite categories in different--not the same--aspects of its nature. "The law of contradiction," he holds (quoting Cohen), "does not bar the presence of contrary determinations in the same entity, but only

requires . . . a distinction of aspects . . . in which the
contraries hold."[53] Hartshorne explains that the dipolar
categories are related to each other by the fact that one
set of categories is contained within its polar opposite.
The more abstract categories are elements within the more
concrete. A man's being or character, for example, is
contained within the sequence of his concrete experiences
as their common factor. Accordingly, through a temporal
sequence of experiences, a man displays a more or less
constant character. God differs only by the fact that his
absolute existence and intrinsic character are a priori
necessities and fully steadfast.

The final criticism (noted above) challenges the
startling implication of the conception of God in process
thought, that God needs some world. The point process
thinkers make is that God, apart from some world, is an
abstraction from his full reality. Without a world, God
would have no concrete experience of some "other," that is,
no data for his physical pole (Whitehead), no concrete
actuality (Hartshorne). As such, he would be merely a
monopolar abstraction, having only a mental pole
(Whitehead) or abstract existence (Hartshorne). Hartshorne
insists, accordingly, that God's essence or character, that
is, his very existence, may be eternally necessary, but he
"cannot be independent of relativity in every sense."[54]
It is hardly surprising, accordingly, that process thinkers
reject the doctrine of creation ex nihilo. They refuse to
speculate about a first divine creative act, taken in a
temporal sense, for it is inconsistent with God's
dipolarity to conceive of a time when God existed without
some "other." God is defined in terms of some world,
though not necessary this particular world. Creation is
not ex nihilo, but emerges out of previous materials, each

preceding phase having been, however, created by God. This
implies, to be sure, an "infinite regress" of matter
created by God; yet in Hartshorne's opinion, while this may
be "unimaginable," it is not demonstratively incoherent:
"all attempts to show this idea to be self-contradictory
seem to have failed." It is, furthermore, far more viable
than the doctrine of creation _ex_ _nihilo_, for a "first
moment of time would be an ontological lie;"[55] "the idea
of a beginning of time is self-contradictory. . . . Even a
beginning is a change, and all change requires something
changing that does not come to exist through that same
change. The beginning of the world would have to happen _to_
something other than the world."[56] We can "no more admit
a beginning of the temporal as such than of God
himself."[57]

While God is defined as always having some "other" as
the object of his experience, this, however, does not
necessarily deny his freedom in regard to his creatures.
Hartshorne points out that God is free in the sense that
there is no external force which compels him to lure the
"other" into ever-increasingly complex states. Nor indeed
is there any "presupposed 'stuff' alien to God's creative
work; but rather everything that influences God has already
been influenced by him." God "is never confronted by a
world whose coming to be antedates his own entire
existence."[58] "Any particular concretum presupposes
divine activity as _antecedent_ _condition_ of its coming to
be."[59] The world (that is, the "other" in God's
experience) is not to be understood as "a second primordial
and everlasting entity over against rather than created by
God;"[60] rather, the world is internal to God and part of
his own reality. "God," writes Hartshorne, "is the
self-identical individuality of the world somewhat as a man

is the self-identical individuality of his ever-changing systems of atoms." Consequently, the "only everlasting (and primordial) entity upon which God acts in creation is himself; all individuals, other than himself, which are influenced by his actions are less than everlasting, or at least less than primordial."[61] Thus, it is "not as if the given world [or its antecedent states] . . . were simply imposed upon God from without as something alien."[62] Rather, all created realities arise "out of potentialities, essences or natures of all things, as embraced eternally in the divine essence."[63] God, in sum, is the ontological ground, the sine qua non, without which no creation could exist.

This particular argument of Hartshorne, as I understand it and have presented it, is typically and undeniably impressive. And yet it is not altogether clear to me that his position is fully viable. On the one hand, he insists that something other than God eternally and necessarily exists, while at the same time insisting that this something other is necessarily dependent upon God for its existence and is eternally part of the divine essence. There obviously is required here a lengthy and detailed justification to make clear why this is not in fact contradictory. I do not think Hartshorne has ever fully or systematically presented such a justification.[64]

Chapter 7: GOD AS PERSUASIVE

A major focus of the process thinkers' critique of traditional Christian theism is directed against its conception of divine power. Whitehead condemned the traditional doctrine for making God a tyrant,[65] dictator,[66] despot,[67] "the one supreme reality omnipotently disposing a wholly derivative world,"[68] "the supreme agency of compulsion:"[69]

> When the Western world accepted Christianity, Caesar conquered, and the received text of Western theology was edited by his lawyers . . . . The brief Galilean vision of humility flickered throughout the ages, uncertainly. In the official formulation of the religion, it has assumed the trivial form of the mere attribution to the Jews that they cherished a misconception about their Messiah. But the deeper idolatry, of the fashioning of God in the image of the Egyptian, Persian, and Roman imperial rulers, was retained. The Church gave unto God the attributes which belonged exclusively to Caesar.[70]

But is not its all-powerful God a far cry from the vision presented by Jesus in the Gospels, "the Galilean origin of Christianity," which "dwells upon the tender elements in the world, [and] which slowly and in quietness operate by love"?[71]

Process thinkers contend that just as it is inconsistent for classical theists to argue that a wholly necessary and unchanging God can know and love a contingent world (see Chapter 6), so likewise is it inconsistent to argue that a wholly necessary and all-powerful God can create a contingent world.[72] Both God's freedom and the world's are negated by the traditional conception of God: "If God is wholly necessary, then so are his acts of creation, and creation can in no sense be described as a free or contingent act."[73] Nor can creaturely acts and decisions be anything but fully determined by the divine necessity. Since God's nature is absolutely necessary, the objects of his knowledge must likewise be necessary.[74]

It is, of course, a contentious issue as to whether the traditional conception of God is as inconsistent with creaturely freedom as process thinkers insist. Yet it is indisputable that the traditional conception of God's omnipotence has in fact been interpreted by many, perhaps a majority of thinkers, as so absolutely all-pervasive that God is understood either to directly cause all events or at least to have the power to intervene. The traditional conception of divine omnipotence, furthermore, has been a major factor in the atheistic protest of such thinkers as Nietzsche, Camus, Sartre, and a veritable host of others, all of whom have felt pressed to choose between belief in such a God and human free will. I do not propose to deal with this issue at length, but wish merely to refer briefly to the work of process theologian David Griffin, who has written a detailed critique of the conception of divine omnipotence as it is represented by the major figures in Christian theological reflection.[75] Griffin's analysis is, to my mind, not only accurate and convincing, but is aptly representative of the process thinkers' position, and the most elaborate study to date of this issue.

DIVINE POWER IN TRADITIONAL THEISM

Griffin contends that the conception of divine power
(and other divine attributes) in St. Augustine's writings,
for example, renders highly dubious the reality of
creaturely autonomy. Augustine's God, defined as
immutable, "is not affected by anything," and as
omniscient, effectively ensures that "there can be no
increase in the content of the divine knowing."[76]
Creatures cannot do other than such a God has eternally and
necessarily foreseen:

> Free choice . . . is not compatible with an
> omniscient being who knows the details of what is
> still the future for us. If this being knows
> infallibly that next year I will do A, instead of
> B or C, then it is necessary that I will do A.
> It may seem to me then as if I make a real choice
> among genuine alternatives, but this will be
> illusory. I really could not do otherwise. If I
> were to do otherwise, God's immutable, infallible
> knowledge would be in error, and this is
> impossible. So in what meaningful sense will I
> be responsible for that choice?[77]

Griffin, accordingly, concludes that Augustine's assurances
(which are, of course, vitally necessary for his theodicy),
that human beings are free and morally responsible agents,
are "purely verbal."[78] They are, in fact,
unsubstantiated and virtually negated by his conception of
God.

If it is countered here that the reason we shall
necessarily decide to do a certain thing at some future
moment is because of our characters, rather than because of
an external compulsion (divine or otherwise), the same
objection, nevertheless, must be made.[79] The argument

that our acts derive from our characters misses the point that, as far as traditional theism is concerned, we are no more responsible for our characters than we are for our individual acts. Our characters, after all, are formed by the choices we make; and yet God eternally and immutably knows--and thus determines--these choices.

Augustine informs us, furthermore, that God's omnipotent will is not impeded by the will of any creature, for God "is not truly called Almighty if He cannot do whatsoever He pleases, or if the power of His almighty will is hindered;" "the will of the Omnipotent is never defeated." "Nothing, therefore, happens but by the will of the Omnipotent, He either permitting it to be done, or Himself doing it."[80] Yet note that whether God directly causes something to happen or merely allows it to happen, the point remains that it happens only because God has willed it. "For it would not be done did He not permit it (and of course His permission is not unwilling, but willing);"[81] and "if He wills it, it must necessarily be accomplished."[82] Augustine contends, moreover, that God "sets in motion even in the innermost hearts of men the movement of their will, so that He does through their agency whatever He wishes to perform through them."[83]

Augustine argues, nevertheless, that both God and the creature have a role in every creaturely free act; yet in attempting to explain how this occurs he suggests that God in fact causes us to do what we do: "we may understand both that we do them, and that God makes us do them, as He most plainly says by the prophet Ezekiel. For what is plainer than when He says, 'I will cause you to do'? . . . . God promises that He will make them to do those things which He commands to be done."[84] Yet how can this be? "Is it not self-contradictory," as Griffin contends,

"and therefore simply nonsense to say that an act is B's
act if the act was totally determined by A?"[85] Augustine,
in sum, may _assert_ that God's causative power does not
render creaturely freedom invalid, but surely such
assertions are unjustified.

Augustine's all-important _free_ _will_ _solution_ to the
problem of evil, accordingly, is problematic, for
creaturely freedom, it would seem, cannot be accounted for
vis-à-vis the divine omnipotent causality. Augustine
attributes all evil to the free will of human beings, or
more precisely, both to the free will of human beings and
to God's punitive action for our misuse of that free will:
"An evil will . . . is the cause of all evils," and God's
"just judgment" is the cause of our having to suffer from
its consequences.[86] Augustine, however, has great
trouble in explaining why the first human creatures,
created perfectly, would abuse their free will. He has
great trouble also in explaining why one-third of the
angelic realm supposedly "fell" from grace. He attributes
the latter to a divine predestination: God withheld his
grace from the angels who fell.[87] And as for the fall of
the first human beings, Augustine suggests that their abuse
of free will was a decision freely chosen by them. And yet
why a sinless Adam and Eve (Augustine, of course, like most
others over the centuries, took the Genesis account as
literal history) would fall is, in essence, left
unexplained. As for the descendants of Adam and Eve,
Augustine attributes the misuse of free will to the
"original sin" inherited from the first human pair. God,
however, saves a chosen few, and by withholding his grace
from the others, they apparently cannot do other than
sin.[88] All of this is, in the minds of process thinkers
(and others, surely), thoroughly confusing and inadequate

as a basis for a solution to the theodicy issue. And yet, it is no secret that the Augustinian theodicy has exerted a predominating influence in traditional Christian theological reflection regarding the problem of evil.[89]

The writings of St. Thomas Aquinas have been no less influential. His conception of God closely resembles Augustine's, and, like his predecessor, he insisted that his understanding of God does not undercut the reality of creaturely freedom. It was argued above, however, that the immutable and independent God of traditional Christian theology (perhaps most comprehensively developed in the writings of Aquinas, and continuingly influential because of its sanction by the Roman Catholic Church) renders suspect God's knowing and loving of the contingencies of the world. It is equally problematic whether creatures have genuine freedom vis-à-vis such a God. Aquinas, of course, offers various complex and often ingenious arguments to substantiate his position. He contends, for example, that just as a man might forsee that a traveller on a road is about to be robbed does not mean that the man caused the robbery, so is it with God's forseeing of future contingent events: he does not cause them by forseeing them. But, as Griffin has pointed out, this analogy is illegitimate since God's forseeing, unlike that of the man's, is necessary and immutable. As such, God's forseeing is the cause of the act forseen.[90]

Aquinas' doctrine of primary and secondary causation seems to fare no better. Every event, according to St. Thomas, has two causes: God as primary cause and the creature as secondary cause. Aquinas' argument is that secondary causes are not negated by God's primary causation. But process thinkers protest that this defence of creaturely freedom is in fact inconsistent with the

doctrine of God espoused by Aquinas and other traditional
theologians. Hartshorne comments:

> in spite of what Thomists say, it is impossible
> that our act should be both free and yet a
> logical consequence of a divine action which
> "infallibly" [eternally and necessarily] produces
> its effects. Power to cause someone to perform
> by his own choice an act precisely defined by the
> cause is meaningless.[91]

While Augustine and Aquinas sought to defend the
reality of creaturely freedom despite their doctrine of
God, some traditional theologians have drawn what process
thinkers regard as the more valid conclusion--given the
traditional conception of God. They openly teach that
creatures, in fact, have no freedom vis-à-vis the divine
causal agency. Martin Luther is a prime example of this
position. He writes, in debate with Erasmus:

> You declare that the will of God is to be
> understood as immutable, yet you forbid us to
> know that his foreknowledge is immutable. Do
> you, then, believe that he foreknows without
> willing or wills without knowing? If his
> foreknowledge is an attribute of his will, then
> his will is eternal and unchanging, because that
> is its nature; if his will is an attribute of his
> foreknowledge, then his foreknowledge is eternal
> and unchanging, because that is its nature. From
> this it follows irrefutably that everything we
> do, everything that happens, even if it seems to
> happen mutably and contingently, happens in fact
> nonetheless necessarily and immutably, if you
> have regard for the will of God. For the will

of God is effectual and cannot be hindered
. . . . Now if his will is not hindered, there is
nothing to prevent the work itself from being
done, in the place, time, manner, and measure
that he himself both foresees and wills.[92]

Luther draws the explicit conclusion that human beings have
no free will:

For if we believe it to be true that God
foreknows and predestines all things, that he can
neither be mistaken in his foreknowledge nor
hindered in his predestination, and that nothing
takes place but as he wills it (as reason itself
is forced to admit), then on the testimony of
reason itself there cannot be any free choice in
man or angel or in any creature.[93]

For Luther, God can foreknow nothing contingently, since
"He foresees and purposes and does all things by his
immutable, eternal, and infallible will."[94] "His will
can neither be resisted nor changed nor hindered."[95]

John Calvin agrees that God "so regulates all things
that nothing takes place without his deliberation." God
"regulates all things according to his secret plan, which
depends solely upon itself."[96] All things are caused by
God's decree and are therefore necessary: what God has
determined must necessarily take place. God has
predestined all things: "God not only foresaw the fall of
the first man, and in him the ruin of his descendants, but
also meted it out in accordance with his own decision."[97]
Human beings, according to Calvin, have no freedom
vis-à-vis God, and yet human beings supposedly are
responsible for their sinful acts! "Man falls according as
God's providence ordains, but he falls by his own
fault."[98] This perplexing doctrine (foreshadowed in

Augustine) is explained by John Hick: "the sinner, whose
fallen nature is such that he necessarily wills wrongly and
who cannot, with his perverted nature, will rightly,
remains nevertheless a free and responsible agent; for he
is acting voluntarily and not from external
compulsion."[99] Our acts are free because they arise from
our own characters; and yet God has preordained that
character! But surely this is unconvincing; is it not
simply a contradiction to argue that God causes all things
and yet that we are free and responsible agents?[100]

GOD AS PERSUASIVE POWER

The understanding of God in process thought differs
greatly from the traditional Christian conception. Rather
than conceiving God as a coercive, all-determining power,
his causal agency is understood to be a "persuasive lure."
This effectively resolves the problem of reconciling
creaturely freedom and divine power. God is "a persuasive
agency and not a coercive agency"[101] who operates with an
"absence of force,"[102] thereby permitting a real and
significant creaturely freedom. Hartshorne insists that
this understanding of God, largely attributable to
Whitehead, "is one of the greatest of all metaphysical
discoveries."[103] God guides all things "by the
persuasiveness of his sensitivity;" his power "is the power
of sensitivity, the power of ideal passivity and
relativity, exquisitly proportioned in its responsiveness
to other beings."[104] God's role (in part) is to provide
every creature with an "initial subjective aim" as a lure
toward ideal and novel possibilities, possibilities which
the creature may or may not wish to actualize. If God's
ideals are actualized, the creature will experience the

maximum value and intensity that was possible at that
particular moment; if the creature chooses not to actualize
the ideals presented by God, there is loss of value and
intensity, and the creature is the lesser for it. So
indeed is God the lesser, since he constantly seeks ever
greater value and intensity in his creatures as important
contributions to his own ongoing experience. Higher-level
creatures (that is, human beings) are capable of
consciously accepting or rejecting God's lure. Lower-level
creatures, however, lacking our mental sophistication, have
relatively less awareness of God's lure and, hence, less
ability "except to act in accordance"[105] with it. There
is, nevertheless, always some aspect of freedom--or at
least "signs of spontaneous activity"--[106]in the
creature, for, as Hartshorne insists, no causal data,
including God, "can absolutely determine a response."[107]
God's lure is a "stimulus"[108] which "determines what
creatures can do, but only they determine what they do
do."[109] God's lure may be the dominant element of the
causal nexus out of which creatures form new experiences,
but it is not the sole element (in a coercive or
all-determining sense). For besides God's lure, there is
the creatures' immediate world and the creatures'
self-autonomy, both of which also contribute to their
selection of those facets of the causal nexus they desire
as ingredients in their new experiences.

IS GOD'S POWER LIMITED?

There are a number of critical issues which emerge
from the process thinkers' understanding of God as a
persuasive power. It is a common criticism, for example,
that process theism invalidly limits God's power: if God is
less than all-powerful, as traditionally conceived, is he

really the God of absolute perfection which alone is worthy
of worship? Hartshorne, however, has responded to this
critique by insisting that, despite the traditional
doctrine of divine omnipotence and causal agency,

> God neither will nor could monopolize
> decision-making, for this is logically
> impossible. Theologians have generally agreed
> that God cannot do the logically impossible, for
> to do that is not really to do anything . . . .
> One does not limit God's power by refusing to
> attribute this nothing to him. To have creatures
> without freedom would be to have creatures which
> are not creatures. Divinity is supreme freedom.
> The absolute negation of freedom is not
> creaturehood but nonentity. Creaturehood is
> precisely the status of freedom lacking the
> supreme qualities of divine freedom. Between
> divine freedom and zero freedom there is plenty
> of room for all possible creatures. Those who
> think otherwise have a strange view of divine
> freedom! One or two steps down from it, they seem
> to suppose, lands one in no freedom. How
> illogical! Any number of steps down can still
> leave some freedom.[110]

Divine power implies, by definition, that God exerts his
causal influence over something; but if this something were
powerless, divine power over it would be meaningless, for
it would be power over nothing at all:

> Instead of saying that God's power is limited,
> suggesting that it is less than some conceivable
> power, we should rather say: his power is
> absolutely maximal, the greatest possible, but
> even the greatest possible power is still one

power among others, is not the only power. God
can do everything that a God can do, everything
that could be done by "a being with no possible
superior."[111]

Rather than being the sole, all-determining causative
power, God's persuasive power inspires freedom in his
creatures and seeks to "maximize opportunities for good and
minimize risks of evil."[112] To insist, on the contrary,
that divine "omnipotence is the power to do anything that
could be done is to equivocate or talk nonsense. There
could not be a power to 'do anything that could be done.'
Some things could only be done by local powers; some only
by cosmic power:"[113]

> We are what we are, not simply because divine
> power has decided or done this or that, but
> because countless non-divine creatures (including
> our own past selves) have decided what they have
> decided. Not a single act of a single creature
> has been or could have been simply decided by di-
> vine action. In the cosmic drama every actor, no
> matter how humble, contributes to the play some-
> thing left undetermined by the playwright.[114]

PERSUASIVE AND COERCIVE POWER

The argument of process thinkers, then, is that the
conception of God as acting solely persuasively (in
contradistinction to the coercive God of traditional
Christianity) is a viable and adequate view, in no way
limiting the divine perfection. Yet despite the fact that
this doctrine of divine persuasive power is a central tenet
of process thought and crucial to process theodicy (as we
shall see), there is some question in my mind as to whether

it has been consistently and adequately presented in the
writings of process thinkers. The writings of Hartshorne,
in particular, seem somewhat problematic at this point, for
despite his explicit insistence that God acts solely
persuasively, much of what he otherwise says about that
persuasive power appears to be more appropriately defined
as coercive! There is little by way of explicit and
systematic definitions of "persuasive" and "coercive" power
in the process literature—an astonishing fact, bearing in
mind that these concepts are of such central importance to
process theism. At the most elementary level,
nevertheless, "persuasive" power may be defined as that
mode of divine power which permits a free creaturely
response, while "coercive" power would deny such a
response. There obviously must be, in the minds of process
thinkers, far more complex definitions of these concepts;
"coercion" perhaps should be more rigorously defined than
simply the limitation of possibility; and, indeed, there
may well be different understandings of "persuasion" and
"coercion" among various process thinkers. Yet my point is
that a full and systematic explication of these concepts
has not yet been accomplished. I would hope to make a
modest contribution toward this needed clarification in the
remainder of this chapter simply by considering some of the
implications of the concepts taken in their most elementary
meanings (as suggested above).[115]

Hartshorne has defined one of God's functions as that
of setting limits to creaturely freedom: "God decides upon
the basic outlines of creaturely actions, the guaranteed
limits within which freedom is to operate."[116] This
divine activity is a persuasiveness: God "must constantly
'persuade' things to obey the laws."[117] "A divine
prehension can use its freedom to create, and for a

suitable period maintain, a particular world order. This
selection then becomes a 'lure,' an irresistible datum, for
all ordinary acts of synthesis."[118] In referring to this
divine activity as a persuasiveness, Hartshorne apparently
believes that it permits a free creaturely response, or, in
other words, that God does not simply coercively negate
creaturely freedom in response. Yet my concern is whether
or not this position is consistent with other statements
Hartshorne has made in reference to the divine imposition
of laws. He argues, for example, that the setting of
cosmic limits to creaturely freedom is solely God's
prerogative. Creatures do not and cannot contribute to the
creation, imposition, or eventual modification of the
limits: "Only God can decide natural or cosmic laws;"[119]
"a multitude of agents could not select a common world and
must indeed simply nullify one another's efforts."[120] God
alone can set limits "which are maximally favorable to
desirable decisions on the part of local agents,"[121] and
indeed, this is one aspect of God's "perfection," namely,
his "wise and efficient limitation of the risks to the
optimum point beyond which further limitation would
diminish the promise of life more than its tragedy."[122]
"Natural laws are the only laws which are always
beneficent . . . . With human laws this may not be so; some
laws create greater risks than opportunities."[123] In
setting and maintaining cosmic limits to freedom, God does
what only he can do for the world:[124]

> Without God . . . individuals could not form even
> a disorderly world, but only a meaningless,
> unthinkable chaos in which there would be neither
> any definite good nor any definite evil. This is
> the same as no world. With God there is an
> order, a world in which good and evil can
> occur.[125]

My interpretation of such passages is that rather than indicating a _persuasive_ causality by God, they imply--clearly against Hartshorne's intention and against the basic spirit of process theism--a divine _coerciveness_, since creatures seemingly have no ability either to create or modify the divinely imposed laws. To be sure, creatures appear to have some degree of freedom _within_ the limits determined by these laws--though Hartshorne's justification of this point will itself be questioned shortly--but the point at issue is his contention regarding the act of imposition itself. We may grant his argument that creatures have freedom not _in spite of_ these laws but _because_ of them (for otherwise there would be only chaos and no world order), yet the fact remains that the laws themselves seem coercively imposed, since their institution was beyond our control and consent. It may be the case, moreover, that the limits are not strictly absolute, since they are "statistical"[126] only, and indeed since God modifies them from time to time,[127] but this would seem to have relevance only for God himself; for creatures, on the other hand, the laws do indeed _appear_ to be statically absolute (and in this sense, coercive) since they remain in effect for countless eons of time with seemingly nothing we can do about them. Finally, with regard to the possible contention that we do not _feel_ coerced by the general laws (for example by gravity) and hence that it may be improper to refer to them as coercive,[128] my point remains that (besides the fact that this does not seem to me to be the case) there is still cause to question Hartshorne's reference to their imposition as being persuasive. For, again, the fact seems to be that the laws were imposed upon us without our consent.

According to Hartshorne, God not only sets the general limits to creaturely freedom, but persuasively lures creatures to the best possible ideals <u>within</u> those general limits. As noted above, Hartshorne contends that God exercises his causal effectiveness in the world by acting as a "stimulus" to which creatures respond (variously, according to their respective levels of mental sophistication).[129] The divine lure is prehended by creatures as an element in their antecedent causal world and, indeed, God is the "supreme" or eminent stimulus therein.[130] All creatures have some awareness of God, though even in man this awareness is not necessarily "clear and distinct," in Descartes' sense.[131] The lower levels of creatures, to be sure, lacking our mental capabilities, have relatively little awareness of God's causal agency and hence have little ability "except to act in accordance" with a divine suggestion, if indeed they feel it consciously at all.[132] That there is, however, always some degree of freedom (or at least spontaneity)[133] is insisted upon by Hartshorne, for no causal stimulus, including God as such, "can absolutely determine a response."[134] He refers to the divine activity, accordingly, as persuasive. God, as stimulus, "determines what creatures can do, but only they determine what they do do." [135] Since man is imperfectly aware of the divine lure, furthermore, Hartshorne can argue that there is "an infinity of ways in which . . . [we] can respond . . . . There is always a variety of ways of falling short of perfection and, therefore, the object cannot of itself determine the imperfect response."[136]

I would suggest, however, that Hartshorne's contention--that this divine luring of creaturely activity is a persuasiveness which, as such, permits genuine freedom

in response--seems to be at odds with much of what he
otherwise says about it. He refers, for example, to the
divine lure as being, at times, unconsciously prehended;
our "awareness" of the lure "need not be conscious in the
sense of being introspectively evident."[137] It is in this
sense that the divine lure is "irresistible,"[138] for
"there must be some mode of divine power which cannot
simply be disregarded."[139] In answer to the question,
furthermore, as to why "the divine fiat [is] so
efficacious," Hartshorne replies: "'Because it offers to
each creature what the creature most wants or appreciates
in the way of intrinsic value.' In short, the fiat is
uniquely eloquent and appealing."[140] For God to obtain
his ideals for us, "to alter us he has only to alter
himself. God's unique power over us is his partly
self-determined being as our inclusive object of
awareness."[141] And indeed, "as this object changes, we
are compelled to change in response."[142] "God molds us,
by presenting at each moment a partly new ideal or order of
preference which our unself-conscious awareness takes as
object, and thus renders influential upon our entire
activity."[143] God inspires us with his "appeal,
attractiveness, or 'charm;'"[144] and this lure is so
relevant to our nature and needs that we cannot "even wish
not to respond:" we "cannot choose but hear."[145] "In the
depths of consciousness we feel and accept the divine
ordering."[146]

It seems to me that such divine activity is not
unambiguously consistent with Hartshorne's thesis that God
acts solely persuasively. Would, for example, a man reject
that which is most attractive and appealing? We would, in
my opinion, have little (if any) inclination not to accept
such a lure, and hence to refer to it as "persuasive" seems

far too imprecise. How are we free, furthermore, in accepting a lure which is "irresistible" or when we prehend God's directive "unconsciously?" How are the lower-level creatures free if they have little (if any) choice "except to act in accordance" with the divine lure? If human beings, moreover, in "the depths of consciousness . . . feel and accept the divine ordering," how are we then free to reject it? Note in this passage that Hartshorne has referred, without further comment, both to our _feeling_ of the lure and our _acceptance_ of it. I would suggest, however, that Hartshorne's failure to clearly distinguish here between what is involved in our _feeling_ of the lure and our subsequent _acceptance_ (or _rejection_) of it is problematic. His basic position seems to be that while the divine lure is innate, that is, universally felt (in varying degrees) by all creatures, it is nevertheless not simply coercively operative in its subsequent acceptance by creatures, especially by the higher creatures (and particularly by human beings). The problem, however, is that Hartshorne (and other process writers) have not made clear the precise details of this position. It is obscure (to me at least) how God's activity can be understood to be solely persuasive in its causal effectiveness when it is said to be _felt_ irresistibly and unconsciously. Why, furthermore, it is not also _accepted_ irresistibly and unconsciously is still to be explained.

There is, of course, no question that Hartshorne vehemently denies that there is any coerciveness exerted by God; but the question I raise is whether this thesis has been established coherently and unambiguously. How _precisely_ are creatures free to respond to God's supposedly persuasive imposition of the natural laws which are the limits to our freedom? And how _precisely_ do creatures respond freely to divine lures which are, for example, unconsciously and irresistibly felt and accepted? Hartshorne's thesis (following Whitehead) that God acts solely persuasively in the world may in truth be "one of the greatest of all metaphysical discoveries,"[147] yet for this thesis to be more generally appreciated, it must be more precisely justified. We need more explicit details of the interaction between God and his creatures; that is, how, precisely, do creatures maintain freedom in their response to God's lure?

It may not be idle to suggest that by insisting that his God acts solely persuasively, Hartshorne and other process thinkers may well be overreacting to their repulsion of the traditional Christian God as a coercive and all-determining force. Perhaps the truth may lie between these two extremes: there may be both coercive and persuasive aspects in God's lure, rather than a sole coerciveness or sole persuasiveness. This point has been hinted at, though without sufficient elaboration, by at least two process thinkers, Norman Pittenger and Daniel Day Williams. They do not, however, seem to have influenced many other process thinkers.[148] Williams' contention is that "coercive aspects... seem as necessary to a real universe as the persuasive aspects," and that accordingly, "no organism would survive five seconds on the exercise of [divine] tenderness alone." He suggests that "Whitehead's doctrine [of persuasive power alone] . . . leads him to ignore the wide ranges of types of force, or coercion, and of mutual interaction. These would seem to have their place [however] in the necessities of being, and therefore require us to find their place in God's being."[149] By ignoring the coercive aspects in God's agency, he insists, "Whitehead has underestimated the disclosure of the divine initiative in religious experience," and thus "has given a partially inadequate account of the relation between God and the world."[150] Williams, interestingly enough, does not extend this criticism to Hartshorne but, rather, asserts that "Dr. Hartshorne is right in stressing also the coercive aspects of our religious experience . . . . There are large coercive aspects in the divine governance of the world."[151] Williams, unfortunately, has not elaborated upon this rather terse observation.

Pittenger likewise has written on this point, and suggested that besides the persuasiveness in Hartshorne's God there is also an aspect of coerciveness. Unlike Williams, however, he extends this thesis to Whitehead as well, arguing that "while God's action in the world is chiefly by lure, solicitation, or loving persuasion, it is not without some measure of coercion, to prevent [the] cosmos from becoming anarchy or chaos." Both Whitehead and Hartshorne, he contends, stress this fact, though "in different ways:" in general, they imply that God is "primarily" persuasive, yet that he is coercive in a secondary way.[152] Pittenger, unfortunately, has not given us more than this brief statement. And while I believe he may be correct, it must be emphasized again that such a position contradicts the explicit statements of Whitehead and Hartshorne, and the apparently firm belief of other process writers, that the process God acts solely persuasively.

There are, I wish also to point out, several passages in Hartshorne's writings which not only imply that God acts coercively at times, but that such coerciveness is both necessary and desirable! God, he writes, "tolerates variety [only] up to the point beyond which it would mean chaos and not a world . . . .[He] prevents reality from

losing all definite character."[153] God must continually
ensure that creaturely freedom does not destroy itself, and
he accomplishes this essential task by restraining our
freedom: "God... set[s] limits by constraint to the
destruction of mutuality,"[154] and he apparently does this
coercively. Hartshorne, in fact, uses that very term:
"Coercion to prevent the use of coercion to destroy freedom
generally is in no way action without social awareness but
one of its crucial expressions. [Hartshorne has defined
divine love as "social awareness and action from social
awareness."] Freedom must not be free to destroy freedom.
The logic of love is not the logic of pacifism."[155]
"Process would come to an end if limits were not imposed
upon the development of incompatible lines of process. The
comprehensive order of the world is enjoyed, but not
determined or created, by ordinary actual entities."[156]

Such passages, in my opinion, are difficult to
construe as being unambiguously consistent with
Hartshorne's conception of a purely persuasive God. Yet
perhaps some light can be shed on this issue. Along with
other process thinkers, Hartshorne conceives God's agency
in the world as a persuasive lure toward the actualization
and enjoyment of new possibilities.[157] Whitehead referred to these possibilities as "eternal objects" and
regarded them as specific, definite ideals contained in the
primordial mind of God. Hartshorne, however, prefers to
define them as an indeterminate range of potentiality which
is not specific until rendered so by creaturely decisions,
and he sees God's causal agency as persuasive in as much as
the creature is free to actualize possibilities within the
limits determined by God through the imposition of the
natural laws. I have suggested that these limits seem to
be coercively imposed since (among other things) the

creature has no choice except to act within the range of possibilities determined by the limits. At this point, however, I think that a distinction ought to be made between the general limits to creaturely freedom imposed by God (that is, the basic laws of nature for a particular cosmic epoch) and the more specific limits which affect creaturely decisions at each particular moment. All creatures, for example, are restricted by the general limitations imposed by the law of gravity, but each creature is also limited more specifically by the restrictions imposed upon it by its particular circumstances in the world. What the creature has done in its past sequence of experiences largely determines the limits of possibilities for its future acts and decisions. As a Canadian, for example, I cannot become President of the United States; this possibility is outside the range of possibilities which have been determined by my past actions and, indeed, by the limitations imposed by my particular social environment. As Lewis Ford puts it (interpreting Hartshorne): "[p]ast occasions restrict the freedom of creaturely activity by imposing limits upon what it can become, for it can only become that which incorporates the past 'given' to it within itself."[158] Hartshorne's point is just this. He writes: "always a particular character is covered by some range of possible diversity (rather than a mere diversity of possibilities, strictly speaking) within which range something must happen . . . . At an earlier moment, taking the world up to then, a [slightly] different range was open for compulsory decisions."[159]

It is important to note here that despite the fact that all creatures are restricted by both general and specific limits, there is in both cases ample room for the freely creative actualization of possibilities and,

accordingly, for persuasive luring by God. Hartshorne
suggests, however, that the range of freedom within these
limits is virtually "infinite,"[160] and this is an
assertion I find difficult to accept. I am willing to
concede that Hartshorne's position might appear to be borne
out by the mathematical fact that between the numbers, say,
1 and 2, there is an infinity of fractions. There are,
furthermore, other possibilities (an infinity of such)
outside the range determined by the numbers 1 and 2: the
fractions, for example, between the numbers 2 and 3. Yet,
I for one find this an obscure and unhelpful notion of
"infinity:" it is limited in one sense, but unlimited
variation is, nevertheless, apparently accounted for! I do
not believe, furthermore, that Hartshorne's position is
helpful when we are considering not just mathematical
possibilities, but the range of possibilities open to
creatures vis-à-vis God's lure and vis-à-vis their physical
environment. Can we have available an infinite range of
possibilities when we are, in fact, restricted by specific
limits? I do not see how this can be. And yet, perhaps
Hartshorne partially escapes this apparent dilemma by
suggesting that while the possibilities within a certain
range may be infinite, those which (when actualized) would
be of significant value are undoubtedly limited, for beyond
a certain number triviality would set in.[161] There is,
nevertheless, a need for greater clarification of this
particular issue.

But the central issue which concerns us at the moment
is to comprehend how God's causal agency operates in the
world, that is, with what degree of persuasive and/or
coercive power. I have pointed out that despite
Hartshorne's insistence to the contrary, his God seems to
have coercively imposed the natural laws which are the

general limits to our freedom. And as for his God's luring
of creaturely acts <u>within</u> the confines of these general
limits, my point is that many of Hartshorne's references to
what are supposedly divine persuasive acts, seem in fact to
imply a divine coerciveness. Hartshorne, to be sure, has
argued vehemently against any type of absolute determinism
(divine or otherwise) and he most surely would not wish his
own position to be interpreted as deterministic. For my
part, I am not suggesting that Hartshorne's God <u>is</u>
coercive--except in so far as the imposition of the general
limits is concerned; but I do suggest that he has not
adequately substantiated his claim that God acts solely
persuasively in reference to the divine luring within these
limits, at each specific moment in creaturely life. With
respect to the imposition of the general limits, I should
think it would be difficult to comprehend how there could
be a world order at all if it were not established
coercively by God. I do not see how creatures themselves
(and more particularly, how inert matter itself, before the
advent of more developed life) could have formed a world
order, although there are those who would not find this
possibility implausible. Whitehead's view, defended by
Lewis Ford and others, that the laws of nature are in fact
not imposed but, rather, are "immanent," seems to me
unacceptable; but this issue is very much an open one and
demands further attention.[162]

Equally demanding of attention is an understanding of
God's causal agency in luring creaturely acts and decisions
<u>within</u> the confines determined by the general limits. The
divine lure cannot be one of absolute coercion, of course,
since this would render virtually unreal any genuine
creaturely autonomy in response to it. The question,
however, is whether the divine lure operates solely

persuasively or perhaps with a _mixture_ of persuasion and
coercion. Hartshorne and the great majority of process
thinkers insist upon the former of these options, and yet
this view must still be reconciled with several references
in Hartshorne's writings which appear to contradict it
(and, for that matter, responses to the argument that some
coercion is necessary must still be more convincingly put
forth).[163] One could, I suppose, simply disregard those
references in Hartshorne's writings which suggest that God
does in fact act somewhat coercively as misleading and un-
fortunate lapses in Hartshorne's logic. Or perhaps one
could apply these references not to God's causal activity
at each specific moment in creaturely life but only to his
act of imposing the general limits for this particular
cosmic epoch. Or, better still, it might be possible to
show by carefully developed arguments that the references
in question are, in fact, consistent with a divine persuasiveness, as Hartshorne has insisted all along. The
precise workings of this divine agency in creaturely life,
to say the least, will be difficult to define; yet in a
preliminary way, we might consider the possibility that
God's lure, perhaps, is "irresistibly" and unconsciously,
persuasively effective to a degree which is directly cor-
related to the creature's openness to it. Perhaps God's
lure is effective to the point of being coercive (though
never absolutely so) somewhat in the way we are affected by
the influence of a dominating personality.[164] Furthermore, with regard to sub-human creatures, those which lack
our conscious free will, perhaps the divine lure is somehow
operative within the creature's very instinctual
capacities.[165] This great lacuna must obviously be more
fully attended to--for it lies at the very heart of process
theism. It will, however, be a most complex and speculative

study, for the precise workings of God's causal agency are hardly something which can be readily and systematically understood. God's lure operates not merely as an element in the causal data of each creature but, rather, operates within the inner recesses of the creature's very instincts and, in the human case, within both our consciousness and (even more so) our non-verbal intuitions.

One final note: I wish to point out that this issue as to whether God operates solely persuasively or with a mixture of persuasion and coercion has rather important implications for the theodicy issue. One question to be addressed in the following chapter, for example, is whether God intervenes (that is, with coerciveness) to prevent certain potentially destructive lines of process from occurring, or to prevent particular instances of evil and suffering. I have already made note of Hartshorne's references to God's apparently coercive act of limiting certain lines of process (though he would insist that only persuasion is employed by God), and I shall later resume discussion of this issue in reference to the question of miracles. Does God miraculously intervene in creaturely affairs to prevent certain evils? The traditional view generally assumes that he does, but my interpretation of Hartshorne is that his references to God's apparent intervention to prevent certain threatening lines of process are misleading if they are taken to imply that God coercively intervenes in specific creaturely situations. This would mean, of course, that there is no ultimate guarantee that good will prevail or, for that matter, that the present world order will survive. But this is not necessarily an impossible position to accept. The ultimate value and meaning of creaturely life is not to be found in human survival on earth or in securing ultimate (post mortem) fulfillment but, according to the process view, in contributing whatever we can--while we are alive--to God's eternal experience. God may coercively impose the general laws for each cosmic epoch and thereby ensure that there will be a world in which great goods are possible, but to hold that God coercively intervenes in specific situations to prevent the occurrence of certain evils is not necessarily the most viable position to take.[166] We shall resume this discussion in the following chapter.

PART THREE: PROCESS THEODICY

The previous two chapters discussed the process thinkers' conception of God as a dipolar, socially interdependent and processing reality, a God which is open to and affected by the world and which, in turn, exerts an effective, persuasive influence upon the world's creatures. This understanding of God plays a central role in process theodicy, as we shall now see. Process thinkers, for example, utilize the free will defence, and insist that their conception of God escapes the apparent contradictions and inconsistencies which plague the traditional versions of this explanation for evil (Chapter 8). Process thinkers also employ an aesthetic explanation for evil, again closely related to their conception of God: it is, they insist, mistaken to think that God could only have created an ordered utopia, or that a world totally devoid of discord and suffering is the only creation consistent with a God of perfect love and power (Chapter 9). All life necessarily seeks and requires aesthetic value, value which is both intense and harmonious, and such value can only be attained by avoiding the aesthetic extremes not only of an absolute chaos and discord, but also of an absolute order. Process thinkers, finally, contend that God "overcomes" evil, though this does not imply that the evil we suffer here and now will be eradicated or that God will intervene (coercively) to prevent its occurrence, even the most ghastly of evils. Nor does it imply that we shall "live on" forever in some post mortem utopia (Chapter 9).

Chapter 8: EVIL AND FREE WILL

A central feature of process theodicy is its defence of the free will solution. Process thinkers reject, however, the traditional version of this solution, arguing that despite the persistent efforts of past theologians to account for creaturely freedom, the traditional conception of God as the all-determining causal force renders creaturely freedom virtually unreal. If, furthermore, the traditional conception of God is softened (as it often is) to hold not that God causes all worldly events but merely permits them, process thinkers protest that this still seriously misconceives the nature of the divine reality, implying that God could prevent worldly events when he sees fit (see above). From the perspective of process thought, creaturely freedom is not understood as an attribute which creatures may or may not have and it is not something which can be superseded by God when he so desires. It is, rather, a metaphysical necessity that all creatures have some degree of freedom, or at least some level of spontaneity which renders inapplicable a strict and absolute causal determinism of events, including a divine determinism: no creaturely act can be fully determined by causes external to the creature, whether these causes are other creatures, the world, or God himself.

Relevant here are the implications of our earlier discussion of the process thinkers' contention that the world was not created by God ex nihilo. Creatures are

co-eternal with God and, as such, have some degree of
independence--though to be sure, without God's lure (if
this were even possible) there would not have been, or
continue to be, an evolutionary advance in this present
cosmic epoch from the insignificant levels of being which
once existed in a state of chaos to the more and more
sophisticated creatures (notably human beings) which now
populate the earth.   In seeking ever new values, ever new
intensities and complex harmonies (see Chapter 9), God
freely and lovingly guides the evolutionary process, and
those values which creatures achieve become part of his own
experience.   At the same time, creatures continually,
though imperceptibly, gain more and more independence from
God, as human beings in particular develop ever-greater
mental capabilities and freedom.

PSYCHICALISM

Process metaphysics contends that all beings are
sentient, to some degree at least, depending upon their
level of mental development. This "psychicalism" (or
"panpsychism")[1] is in direct contradiction of the
alternatives of materialism and dualism, the latter
implying a "division of substances into those which do and
those which do not possess a soul,"[2] and the former
positing "the existence of atoms, [as] discontinuous,
discrete, independent bits of matter, devoid of feeling and
life, isolated except for accidental external relations,
timeless and unchanging with respect to internal
constitution and hence without growth or evolution."[3]
The concept of "mere matter" has been shown to be
superfluous by modern scientific advances and by the
philosophical arguments of Leibniz, Bergson, Peirce,
Whitehead, Hartshorne, and others.[4] The dualism which

understands mind and matter to be two ultimately distinct
sorts of entities is rejected by process thinkers in favor
of a view which interprets mind and matter as "two ways of
describing a reality that has many levels of
organization."[5]

Process thinkers conceive of the ultimate or basic
"reals" which constitute all creatures as microscopic and
momentary instances of energy[6] (Whitehead's so-called
"actual entities" or "actual occasions") which contain both
mental and physical characteristics.[7] These actual
entities form the various macroscopic groupings which
appear to our sense perception as, for example, rocks,
animals, trees and human beings (see above, Chapter 6). It
is such groupings, or rather the interrelationships among
these entities, which constitute spatial and temporal
extension. And it is the sentience of the more complex
groupings ("societies") of actual entities which accounts
for the free and spontaneous "creative advance" of the
world. At every instant, all creatures (that is, the
myriad of actual entities which form the macroscopic
groupings) are in the continual process of synthesizing
("concrescing") the data of their immediate environment
into new experiences. Each creature is dipolar, having
both a mental and a physical pole. The physical pole
mainly repeats the creature's past physical
characteristics; that is, it repeats the basic physical
pattern of the actual entities which constitutes it as a
creature. But the mental pole, which has evolved to a more
sophisticated level, is able to do more: it introduces
novelty by internalizing in its experience what previously
had been merely an indeterminate potentiality.

RELATIVE DETERMINISM

Process thinkers reject both absolute indeterminism
and absolute determinism as invalid interpretations of the
world's causality. Hartshorne insists that indeterminism
(mere chance) is mistaken in holding that the antecedent
conditions of an event (that is, of each new creaturely
concrescence) in no way cause the event. For surely the
antecedent conditions cannot be completely irrelevant to
the event. Absolute indeterminacy, which holds that "at
least some events have no causes," is, as Hartshorne
insists, clearly a strawman position, set up by
determinists for easy burning, and "is a doctrine no one
defends, a fictitious position."[8] Yet the absolute
determinist is wrong in insisting that events are fully
implicit in their causal conditions. Hartshorne calls his
alternative position "relative determinism,"[9] and while
he acknowledges that all events must, of course, have
antecedent causes, the point he makes is that these causes
are never the "necessary and sufficient" reason for the
events. There is always an aspect of creativity in the
creature to be considered. The antecedent conditions
predetermine only the limits within which the new
experiences must fall; they cannot predetermine the
experiences to the last detail.[10]

Herein lies the basic distinction between the process
thinkers' position and that which they believe is implied
by absolute or "classical" determinism, and by traditional
Christian views of divine determinism, the view "embodied
in the standard medieval theological view that God knows
the world simply by knowing himself as its cause:"

> The cause was the superior entity, or if not,
> cause and effect were "equal." Effects were to
> be known in their causes, as well as causes in

their effects. And so, before an event existed
to be known it was nevertheless completely
defined and ready to be known. (Or else it
existed before it happened) . . . . Thus an
effect was held to be implied by, logically
contained in, though inferior to its cause, the
cause minus something, and then what is the point
of causal production?[11]

Absolute determinism, then, according to process thinkers,
whether one is referring to the causal determinism of the
world or to the divine finalism of traditional Christian
theism, destroys the rational coherency of the world by
making causes indistinguishable from their effects and by
obliterating temporal succession and freedom:

But then since [according to determinism]
everything is thus logically contained in
everything else, all distinction of ground and
consequence, of fundamental and non-fundamental,
of universal and particular, of logical relations
in general . . . vanishes. Nothing can be more
essential or comprehensive or "eternal" than
anything else in a system in which all things
necessarily enter into the being of all things
. . . . Thus, as Peirce was never weary of
pointing out, absolute determinism applied to the
entire cosmos amounts to sheer nominalism, the
denial of all difference between general and
individual, as well as between possible and
real.[12]

Process thinkers contend that all reality is truly
"becoming," that is, freely creative ("To be is to
create"[13]), such that no creaturely act is simply (that
is, fully) predetermined by the efficient causality of the

world, or indeed, by divine causality. The antecedent conditions of each new experience, however, restrict the new experience to a definite range of possibilities. "Nothing outside the range is to be even possible,"[14] though (as noted in the previous chapter) there is apparently an "infinity" of possibilities within this range that may be actualized:

> every event is caused, that is to say, it issues out of a restricted or real potentiality; but also, every event occurs by chance, that is to say, it is more determinate than its proximate real potentiality, and just to that extent is unpredictable, undeducible from its causes and causal laws.[15]

GOD AND CREATURELY FREE WILL

Having argued that creatures have both sentience and freedom (or at least spontaneity), process thinkers insist that this freedom cannot be negated or rendered illusory by the divine causal agency. Process thinkers, as we have seen, conceive of God's causal activity as persuasive. God sets limits (as does the causal data in each creature's world)[16] within which creaturely freedom must be actualized, but there is an infinity of possibilities open to creatures **within** these limits. Process thinkers postulate, accordingly, that there is a "division of powers,"[17] a mutual influence between God and creatures. God has no monopoly of power, since all creatures have some autonomy. The traditional Christian conception of God as the supreme cause of all things, on the other hand, is misconceived if it is taken to imply that he is so powerful that he controls (or at least could control) creation simply as he wills. Such a conception of divine omnipotence is problematic, for it implies the denial of the very meaning of what a creature is, that is, a being which necessarily has some degree of autonomy. The "minimal solution" to the problem of evil,[18] then, is that responsibility for evil is shared by all beings. That God acts purely persuasively, furthermore, (at least within the limits to freedom which he has imposed) is not something which he could change: it is his fundamental mode of action vis-à-vis creatures whose necessary (though varying) range of creativity rules out any absolute control by any other being, including God himself.

PERSUASIVE AND COERCIVE POWER

At this point, however, we must consider how the free will solution in process theodicy is affected by our previous discussion of the persuasive-coercive aspects of God's causal agency. A purely persuasive God would seem to be consistent with creaturely freedom, but is a partially coercive God? It seems to me that we can answer in the affirmative by noting that despite God's unquestionably significant (that is, effective) causal influence, creaturely autonomy is not necessarily overruled. It is surely not a matter of absolute autonomy versus absolute divine causality. God's causal influence is significant and powerful, but if God were the sole power, he would have power virtually over nothing at all. That there is a coercive aspect of the divine causality, furthermore, can best be understood as his restricting of the range of creaturely freedom via establishing the laws of nature as the limits to freedom. God presumably acts persuasively in luring creaturely acts within these limits. Yet (as I noted in the previous chapter) whether there is also some coerciveness involved in the latter has not been adequately explored in the process literature. And until it is, some critics may find its defence of creaturely free will vis-à-vis divine causality to be as "merely verbal" as process thinkers find aspects of the traditional theodicies. Hartshorne's writings, as they stand, suggest that God controls the possibilities for good and evil, and to such an extent that the possibilities for good always outweigh those for evil (see below). But precisely how God does this solely persuasively, or indeed that with what degree and mixture of persuasion and coercion, is not clear. All we can say with certainty at this point is that—despite the fact that process thinkers have not fully justified it—creatures must be partly free vis-à-vis God and other creatures, for otherwise they would not be creatures. And this implies that creatures themselves, not God alone, are at least partly responsible for the goods and evils in the world. Hartshorne, accordingly, writes:

> The justification of evil is . . . that the creaturely freedom from which evils spring, with probability in particular cases and inevitability in the general case, is also an essential aspect of all goods, so that the price of a guaranteed absence of evil would be the equally guaranteed absence of good . . . . Risk of evil and opportunity for good are two aspects of just one thing, multiple freedom; and that one thing is also the ground of all meaning and all existence. This is the sole, but sufficient, reason for evil as such and in general.[19]

God is not the direct cause of evils; his role, rather, is to ensure that there is a world within which free beings can exercise their creative, partially autonomous powers, and always with great possibilities for good:

> God does not adjust concrete evils and goods in
> some inconceivably wise way; he does not, as far
> as we know, manipulate concrete happenings at
> all. He adjusts basic kinds of possibility of
> good and evil as inherent in certain laws of
> nature. The rest is simply what the creatures
> happen to decide.[20]

The free will solution in process theodicy,
accordingly, is based on the contention that creaturely
freedom is a viable reality only if God is not the actual
or potential all-determining causal factor in creaturely
acts and decisions. If the opposite position, on the other
hand, is in fact what the traditional conception of God
implies, then it seems virtually inconceivable how
creatures can be significantly free and autonomous agents.
And, of course, if creatures are not autonomous, it is
difficult to comprehend not only how they can be considered
creatures at all (rather than merely aspects or attributes
of God), but how there can be moral justice in the fact
that they are to be eternally rewarded or punished for
these acts (as the traditional view holds--though perhaps
not so prevalently as in the past).[21]

DOES GOD INTERVENE?

The traditional conception of God can be softened, to
be sure, to suggest that God does not cause all creaturely
events but merely permits them. Yet if God, on the one
hand, were to refrain from all causal activity (persuasive
as well as coercive) and to permit all moral evil
potentially caused by creatures, the world would,
conceivably, reduce to chaos; and on the other hand, if God
were (coercively) to disallow all moral evil by permitting

only good creaturely acts, creaturely freedom would then be effectively negated. But was it not possible for God to have prevented, if not all moral evil, at least the most ghastly forms of such evil? This would still have permitted a significant range of creaturely autonomy. Indeed, can it not be argued that God has in fact done so, for if he had not, evils far more ghastly and horrendous than those we must now endure would be devastatingly rampant? Perhaps it can, but there are many who would insist that because of the present amount of misery and suffering in the world, it appears very unlikely that God has intervened. Critics like McCloskey, accordingly, insist that since "free will is compatible . . . with less moral evil than actually occurs," this in itself is a strong argument against God's very existence.[22] For if God is able to prevent the most ghastly evils--either by directly intervening or (as will be discussed in detail below) by creating creatures in such a way that we would always use our free will for good ends--why has he not done so? The theist, nevertheless, has an interesting set of options in response, and we must examine these with some care. The theist can insist that God, as noted above, has intervened to prevent the most ghastly evils; or (perhaps more convincingly) the theist can argue that God has not and cannot intervene! While these responses obviously are contradictory, both have been utilized by Christian theologians.

The first option, in fact, brings us to a consideration of the traditional Christian belief in intermittent divine violations of natural laws, miracles, which occur either in response to prayer or because of the divine omniscient initiative. But I would suggest (with many others) that belief in God violating the laws of nature is not without serious problems. Religious

writings, of course, contain innumerable testimonies of
divine interventions, from biblical accounts of God's
guiding his chosen people and of Jesus' nature and healing
miracles, to modern day "faith healings." And while I do
not wish to dispense with these accounts too flippantly,
there are well known naturalistic, existential, and
symbolic interpretations of the biblical miracles which
suggest that they are not necessarily (nor probably)
literal accounts of actual historical events.[23] The
report of Jesus' walking on water, for example, may have
been a purely symbolic literary device to teach the first
century Hebrew that Jesus is the "new creation:" the
reference to walking on water would bring to mind the
Genesis account of the first divine creation, which
involved separating (or calming) the waters of chaos.[24]
Biblical scholars have addressed this issue in great
detail, and to them I refer the reader.

While the nature miracles may, perhaps, be interpreted
this way, I do not, however, wish to suggest that the
healing miracles of Jesus are merely symbolic. After all,
faith healings still occur today, and there is no reason to
believe that Jesus likewise could not have performed such
healings. The issue, however, is how to interpret what
occurs in these healings. It is possible that there are
naturalistic explanations for such cures, the full
understanding of which, unfortunately, is beyond our
present comprehension. Someone who is cured by a faith
healing may believe God has intervened and violated the
laws of nature to relieve him of his agony, yet it is at
least possible that the cure was effected by natural
causes. Perhaps the sick person, under the stimulation
occasioned by faith and trust in the miracle-worker,
activated some as yet unknown power of the body, some

natural immune mechanism, to somehow cure himself. This whole area is highly speculative, to be sure, and at present forbids more precise understanding.[25] Theists, nevertheless, <u>know</u> that God is involved in the world and somehow active and effective in the lives of all beings. They <u>know</u> also that God is somehow involved in the faith healings. But to conceive of the divine causal agency as violating the laws of nature would seem to be a primitive and rather inadequate conception of God's interaction with the world. Process thinkers suggest a more promising alternative.

This brings us to the second option. Theists can argue that God does not intervene by violating his own laws of nature in order to prevent certain evils from occurring, or indeed to eradicate some which have already occurred. To do so would be inconsistent with his omniscience, for to violate his own laws from time to time in "stopgap" fashion would seem to imply that he did not have the power or knowledge to create better and more appropriate laws in the first place. Divine intervention, furthermore, would risk what would appear to us as pure arbitrariness. If God, for example, were to cure one case of cancer, why not another? Indeed, why not them all? The suggestion that the divine cures are in direct response to prayer seems unsatisfactory, for this implies that God can be manipulated by "adequate" prayer. Such a view is surely rather primitive, and one which is hardly appropriate to contemporary theological reflection. It denies, or at least somewhat undermines, furthermore, the long and hallowed Christian belief that God's causal activity is a free gift of grace, not the result of human works. If, moreover, God were to violate natural laws, this would put the very structure of the world in jeopardy. One moment

gravity would be in operation and at the next it would be
superseded by divine fiat in order to prevent some ghastly
evil. This, surely, would render human rationality and
scientific thinking meaningless, for these human activities
(and indeed all human activities) depend upon a stable
natural order.[26]

To argue that God does not prevent evils by miraculous
violations of natural laws must not, however, be taken to
imply that he does not act at all in the world! Process
thinkers conceive of God as constantly "luring" each
creature, at every moment in its life-sequence of
experiences, toward the best possible ends, as determined
by the creature's particular situation. God lures
creatures continually to use their natural powers in order
to make the best of every situation; he does not intervene
merely from time to time in violation of natural laws (or,
indeed, in violation of creaturely freedom), but rather
acts constantly within each creature's very being. Thus,
while traditional Christianity, more often than not,
conceives God as intervening to prevent certain ghastly
evils and suffering (though this view seems to be changing,
as we move further away from biblical literalism and toward
new conceptions of God), this most certainly is not the
only possible, nor indeed most obviously viable, option.
Process thought conceives God's causal agency as operating
within each creature as an effective lure, and this is
accomplished without violating natural laws (and,
presumably, without violating the creature's autonomy).

A question arises at this point, however. Earlier I
argued that Hartshorne's God does, in fact, appear to
intervene in order to ensure that creaturely freedom does
not destroy itself or the world (see Chapter 7). I noted,
furthermore, that Hartshorne has given us very little

information as to exactly what this entails, beyond insisting that the divine causal agency is not coercive. My suggestion to the contrary, nevertheless, is that this agency _does_ seem coercive in as much as Hartshorne's God manipulates the limits of possibilities for free creaturely activity--or so Hartshorne's texts imply to me. But, if this is the case, it is difficult to define precisely how Hartshorne's account differs from the traditional view of divine intervention with which I have just found fault, and which seems incompatible with process thought. The following observation, however, may help to clarify this issue. While the traditional God supposedly intervenes by violating natural laws to prevent certain creaturely decisions and certain natural events--acts of violence, disease, famines--Hartshorne's position, it seems to me, is that God does not intervene to prevent specific evils (this particular case of cancer or that particular drought), but rather that God orders the general laws of nature in such a way that they are conducive always to great possibilities for goods. This ordering, however, does not take place to meet creaturely contingencies, but in a far more general way: God orders the laws of nature for each cosmic epoch. More than this (though including his constant, persuasive luring of the creature from within), God cannot do.

Hartshorne's writings on this important point, it seems to me, are not as clear as they need to be. Many of his references to God's causal agency (see above) seem to imply a coercive intervention not only with respect to the imposing of the general cosmic laws (the natural laws of a particular cosmic era) but with regard to creaturely activity _within_ the general limits established by those laws. My suggestion is that we interpret only God's activity in establishing the general laws as coercive, not

his causal agency within those limits. That God exerts
some coercive power to establish the laws of nature would
seem to be essential for there to be a world at all in
which good and evil are possible. And further, the free
will explanation would not be jeopardized if God's causal
lure within those limits were conceived as anything short
of an absolute coerciveness. I suggested above that
perhaps the effectiveness of God's lure is determined by
our openness to it. The more open we are, the more
persuasive (and indeed the more coercive) it is. I
suggested, moreover, that it is inappropriate to believe
that God coercively intervenes (presumably with an absolute
coerciveness) to prevent specific creaturely events from
occurring, for among other things, such interventions would
seem to be purely arbitrary acts with no justifiable
parameters. It would be inappropriate (if not, in fact,
impossible) for God to overrule creaturely freedom at all,
let alone in such a "stopgap" fashion. Hartshorne's
references, accordingly, which seem to imply the necessity
of divine interventions in specific situations (to prevent
certain potentially threatening and destructive events from
occurring), seem to me to be unhelpful and misleading and
are at odds with the essential spirit of his own process
system.

What this implies for the theodicy issue, of course,
is that there is no guarantee that the world order, as we
know it, will survive. If God does not intervene
intermittently to prevent certain potentially threatening
situations, the world may well be destroyed by natural
forces or, more likely, by human wickedness. I shall argue
later, however, that this possibility, as well as the lack
of a final, good end to the world process, does not count
decisively against God's perfect goodness. For despite the
absence of a final end point where human beings will be

brought to spiritual perfection in some sort of utopic paradise, process thought does in fact account for the ultimate and eternal meaning and value of our lives by means of its doctrine of "objective immortality" (see Chapter 9).

PHYSICAL EVILS

But let us turn now to another aspect of the free will defence in process thought. While traditional theodicy usually attributes only _moral_ evil to human free will, process thought attributes not only moral evil but also _physical_ evil to the free will, or rather, creativity, of all creatures. Process metaphysics holds that a line cannot be drawn between sentient and supposedly lifeless aspects of reality, since all life (from God to the most insignificant level of existence) has at least some degree of creativity. And it is this creativity (spontaneity, relative indeterminacy) which, by the mutual conflict it generates among creatures, causes physical as well as moral evils. Despite the legal system, natural disasters are not "acts of God." These and other physical evils (birth defects, disease, etc.) are not the result of divine providence as tests, trials, punishments, or the like, for while God may be the preeminent and all-pervasive causal agent, "the creatures, in their non-eminent way, are also causes or creators. . . .It, therefore, cannot be deduced from the eminent power of God that what happens is his doing, since the totality of causal conditions of an event includes all antecedent creatures as well as God."[27] Creaturely freedom, writes Hartshorne, is "the necessary counterpart of eminent creativity. With a multiplicity of creative agents, some risk of conflict and suffering is inevitable. The source of evil is precisely this

multiplicity."[28] "From particles to man," in short,
"nothing is simply determined by God."[29] Natural (or
physical) evils are the result of the "frustrations and
sufferings caused innocently by subhuman creatures, or by
human creatures with perfectly good intentions."[30] The
only way to avoid such evils would be to have a world order
in which they could not arise. Yet such an ideal utopia is
surely an absurd possibility, for, as Hartshorne points
out, "God could have determined otherwise than he has the
limits of creaturely causation or power (as seen in the
laws of nature)," but then "he could not have eliminated
the non-eminent creativity" of beings in the world,[31] for
to be genuinely other than God and not merely an attribute
of the divine reality, creatures must have some
independence and autonomy. Hartshorne argues, moreover,
that it is consistent with belief in a God of absolute
perfection to believe also that he has ordered the laws of
nature so as to provide the maximum opportunities for good
and the minimum risk of evil. In a world of genuinely
self-creative beings, the possibility of no evil or
suffering occurring is, quite simply, unrealistic. God's
role "is not to enforce a maximal ratio of good to evil,
but a maximal ratio of chances of good to chances of
evil."[32]

It may, of course, seem incredulous to speak of
spontaneity or indeterminacy at the atomic level, and yet
this fact is borne out by modern physics.[33] Many
physicists attribute this indeterminacy not merely to
temporary or permanent limitations of human knowledge or to
imperfect human measurements, but in fact to an objective
characteristic of nature itself. The indeterminacy in
nature, however, is not to be equated with human freedom.
Both indeterminacy and freedom involve an aspect of

unpredictability, to be sure, yet to make free choices requires conscious awareness. Process thought is committed to the fundamental premise, nevertheless, that all levels of being are governed by the same metaphysical principles. Quantum physics, accordingly, is not irrelevant to the understanding of human freedom, for it establishes the basic indeterminacy involved at all levels of existence: "ethical freedom can, though less simply or conclusively than some perhaps have supposed, derive support from the new physics. For that physics has given up the dream, the pseudo-category, of causality which in principle excludes chance."[34] "Moral freedom . . . is a special, high-level case of the creative leap inherent in all process, the case in which the leap is influenced by consciousness of ethical principles."[35]

At this point I wish to suggest that while it may well be the case that all life exhibits some degree of self-causation, based on an indeterminacy of causes, and while this may indeed result in physical evils due to the mutual conflict to which spontaneous acts give rise, there would seem to be a more readily accessible (and complementary) explanation for physical evils: physical evils can be understood as the inevitable by-products of natural laws, laws which in themselves are great goods and absolutely necessary, since without them there could be no creaturely life, indeed no world, but merely an unstructured chaos. While physical evils may in fact be attributable to the indeterminate spontaneity of sub-human levels of being, it is not always easy to comprehend how this is the case. The hurricanes and famines and droughts, for example, which often cause so much pain and suffering in the world seem more readily explained as necessary by-products of natural laws. For there to be a world at

all, there must be laws, that is, a world order; and it is
inevitable that these laws will cause suffering. The water
that is so essential for life can also kill by drowning;
the fire that secures us from the cold can also burn; the
gravitational pull that ensures an orderly nature can kill
us if we lean too far out of an upper-story window, and so
on.[36]

If, however, it is argued at this point that the very
fact that nature's laws have such unavoidable consequences
for pain and suffering is in itself evidence not of God's
creation of a good world order, but rather of God's lack of
concern (or, indeed, evidence of his nonexistence), the
theist stands on solid ground to respond otherwise. For
without these laws there could be no life other than
meaningless, primitive chaos; it is, moreover,
inappropriate to think that God could intervene to alter
the evil effects of the natural process (as was argued
above). We shall pursue this discussion of the natural
law explanation for evil in the following chapter,
addressing in particular the question as to why God could
not have created a world with an entirely different
structure, one which is less conducive to evil
by-products. But for the present, two or three other
issues which pertain more directly to this chapter's
discussion of the free will solution must be considered.

FREE BEINGS WHO ALWAYS CHOOSE GOOD?

There are critics of the free will solution (whether
it be the traditional version or the process version) who
contend that if God really existed, he could have created
human beings in such a way that we would use our freedom
invariably for good. J. L. Mackie, for example, insists
that God was not faced with the choice between creating

free beings who would inevitably use their free will for evil as well as for good, and creating innocent automata with no freedom, automata which would be conditioned to do only good. There "was open to him the obviously better possibility of making beings who would act freely but always go right."[37] That God did not avail himself of this possibility "is inconsistent with his being both omnipotent and wholly good." Mackie confidently asserts, accordingly, that this observation "is sufficient to dispose of . . . "[the free will] solution."[38]

From the perspective of traditional theology, it seems to me, that in creating the world ex nihilo, God supposedly could have created creatures which were entirely good; is this not what the Genesis account and its traditional interpretation[39] seems to imply? Adam and Eve were created perfectly. Yet, setting aside the issue of the historical literalness of the Genesis account, the question which arises as to how perfect creatures could sin, seems itself unanswerable.[40] Traditional theology insists, to be sure, that the first perfect human pair did indeed sin and, thus, that the possibility of acting solely for good no longer exists for their progeny--unless, of course, Christ's power enables us to use our freedom properly, for good ends! As Augustine has argued, with Christ's grace, we are "not able to sin" (non posse peccare), but without this free and unmerited gift of grace we are "not able not to sin" (non posse non peccare).[41] All of this, however, seems to render problematic any genuine creaturely free will. We cannot act for good ends unless God wills it, and otherwise we must surely act toward evil ends. I see little, if any, free will in this account, and very little which is of use in formulating a response to a critique such as Mackie's. I do not, of course, wish to make light of Augustine's proposal, or its use (in varying forms) in much of traditional theology; but I, for one, find it very unhelpful.

From the perspective of process thought, however, an answer is more readily available. As we have seen, the process God does not create the world ex nihilo, but rather, the world exists (in a primitive, chaotic state, at least) co-eternally with God, and its creatures have some degree of independence and freedom, or at a minimum, rudimentary spontaneity and creativity. It is, accordingly, not possible for God to create creatures which act only for good ends. God must act persuasively in the world, for creatures, as such, are somewhat autonomous (to varying degrees). If God were in fact to act coercively to bring about solely good ends, to do so would be to negate the very reality of the creature! The only way creatures could use their freedom, as Mackie would like, solely for good ends, would be for God to control their decisions and actions. I see no other way which makes any sense. And yet, of course, this would deny creatures any real freedom vis-à-vis God's causality. Human beings, as such, could hardly cultivate moral characteristics, or be anything other than the divine will has determined. And this would mean that we could contribute nothing to God (see below). Indeed, if God were to determine our actions, would this not, as Hartshorne points out, "amount to supposing that the ideal form of the voluntary could be entirely involuntary?"[42] It is difficult to see, moreover, how the world as a whole could be constituted so as to contain only goods: every creature is involved with countless others in a web of life wherein the actions of each creature affect (positively or negatively) the lives of the others. What is good for one is often the cause of evil and suffering in others. It is meaningless, therefore, to think that all creatures could act solely for good ends, and that God, as God, would and could have created the world as such.

FREE BEINGS WITH A BIAS TO GOOD?

I find other closely related criticisms of the free will solution equally unconvincing. McCloskey, for example, has argued that rather than creating human beings such that they would always act toward good ends, God at least "could have created man with a strong bias to good," thereby ensuring that much of the world's evil, that which is caused by us, would not have been produced.[43] Hare and Madden concur in their suggestion that God could have given us a "disposition" to act rightly and thereby to "have avoided the more ghastly consequences of misused freedom."[44] Human beings would "occasionally" choose evil, but more often would be disposed toward good. The minute possibility for choosing evil, however, would ensure our freedom and moral integrity while at the same time eliminate most of the moral evil from the world. That God did not create us as such "seems to argue against [his] all-powerfulness or all-goodness."[45]

This contention, however, seems rather shaky to me. It could be argued, for example, that God has in fact disposed us toward good. I, personally, would not find this proposal to be very helpful, but to accept or reject it with any certainty is clearly somewhat arbitrary. The opposite argument can be made; namely, that a virtuous character cannot simply be instilled in us in much the same way that we put on a suit of clothes. For, as Hartshorne has pointed out, our moral "character is a deposit of past creaturely action,"[46] something which we create only by our sequence of actions and free decisions. Ninian Smart

has argued this point admirably, showing that we could not
have been created wholly good in a world which is itself
wholly good, for such qualities as courage, tolerance,
perseverance, the overcoming of pain and temptation, and so
on, can only be acquired through actual experiences, those
in fact which involve real aspects of physical and mental
pain and suffering.[47]   Human beings, in other words,
cannot be called "good" if they have done nothing to merit
this appellation: "the concept goodness is applied to
beings of a certain sort, beings who are liable to
temptations," who have fears, and undergo struggles against
pain and threatening situations. But "if they were to be
immunized from evil, they would have to be built in a
different way," and this would "mean that the ascription of
goodness would become unintelligible."[48]   The argument
that God could have created us with a strong "bias" to good
seems to miss this point. We cannot have a "bias" to good
which we ourselves have not first developed by our acts and
decisions.

It is here that Pierre Teilhard de Chardin's
evolutionary perspective (or its counterpart in John Hick's
"soul-making" theodicy) seems to be somewhat relevant. God
desires his creatures to act for good ends, and yet we must
slowly and diligently, and often painfully, work toward
bringing about the fulfillment of our spiritual natures.
We must "make our souls" step by step. God could no more
create us (or any other creature) perfectly virtuous "in
the beginning" than a mother can give solid good to a
newborn child.[49]   It is, furthermore, a mistake to think
that a hedonistic paradise is the only world which would
have been created by an all-powerful and all-loving God.
The moral and spiritual natures of human beings must slowly
evolve toward ever higher states, just as our physical and

mental natures slowly evolve. And while there is, of course, no guarantee that our spiritual natures will continually evolve toward more and greater goodness and virtue, we do have this great opportunity, if we respond to the divine lure. Yet, while traditional theology postulates that there is an end to our earthly struggle in heaven, where presumably our spiritual perfection is realized, the process view sees no final end point.[50] The process simply continues, though with greater and greater values achieved and hopefully ever greater spiritual possibilities realized (see Chapter 9).

While, furthermore, process theodicy accepts the main premise of the soul-making view, that moral goodness can be acquired only by overcoming physical evils,[51] process thinkers would reject any ascription of this evil to God's direct agency, as a deliberate goad to soul-making. It is unacceptable to postulate that each and every evil fulfils some specific purpose for good ends. Clearly there are evils which lead not to good ends but to even greater evils. The distribution of evil, moreover, is so apparently unjust that any belief that it is deliberately caused by God for specific ends seems religiously, morally, and intellectually offensive. Many creatures suffer greatly, overly greatly, for the good ends which may result from their suffering; and some evils seem to contribute virtually nothing to the overall good or, for that matter, to any individual's good. It may, of course, be countered here (in defence of a divine determinism of events) that only God can see and appreciate the good ends which every specific evil serves. Yet process thinkers would object that such a view of divine causality not only would be morally objectionable (for every cancer and equally horrendous misery would then be attributed to God), but it would render creaturely autonomy virtually meaningless.

IS FREE WILL WORTH THE RISK OF EVIL?

But let us turn to a final critique of the free will solution; namely, that free will simply is not worth the risk of the evils it causes, that the world's devastating evils are too high a price to pay for the privilege of having freedom. Defenders of the free will solution often argue that "[f]ree will alone provides a justification for moral evil" and that "[t]he goods made possible by free will provide a basis for accounting for moral evil."[52] The critic counters that free will is, in fact, compatible with less or no moral evil, that God could have created human beings with freedom and yet as wholly good. The absurdity of this claim, however, has already been noted. But there is another argument raised by the critics. McCloskey, for example, insists that free will does not justify the evils it causes, since it is logically possible that human beings could use their freedom more for evil than for good, to create an immense chaos of evil and suffering. Should this occur, it would be impossible to think of free will as being such an enormous value that it outweighs this evil.[53] Indeed, even the possibility of this devastation occurring renders the value of free will highly questionable.

I do not, however, find this argument convincing. It is possible that free will could cause absolute havoc in the world, more so perhaps than can even be imagined. And indeed, free will could very well destroy the world and virtually all significant life forms, dissolving the world order back into a primitive chaos of unstructured insignificance. Yet I for one would still insist that having had the free will was worth it, and I would not

expect God to intervene (coercively), for to have existed
without freedom would have been no life at all, at least
not to the extent that it is human life or an equivalent,
significant species of partially autonomous beings. From
the perspective of process thought, furthermore, as we have
seen, the very issue (as to whether it was better for God
to have given us freedom with its great potential for evil
and destruction, rather than no freedom at all) is largely
beside the point. For creatures, as such, necessarily have
some degree of spontaneity and indeterminacy by virtue of
the fact that we <u>are</u> creatures. God has guided the present
world from a level of low-grade chaos to a complex
structure which supports human beings, with great
capacities of free choice. With each major advance in the
evolution and development of this freedom, greater
possibilities for evils also have arisen. Yet this risk is
taken by God in his seeking of ever new values. To think
that absolute order is the ideal to be sought by creatures
or by God is to misunderstand the need to seek and
actualize new values, values which are gained through
struggles and challenges. The following chapter will
address this aspect of process theodicy more fully, and to
it we now turn.

Chapter 9: AESTHETIC VALUE AND THE OVERCOMING OF EVIL

In the first chapter of this section, the process thinkers' contention that evils are attributable to the creativity of the world's creatures was discussed. We may now develop further this central aspect of process theodicy with specific reference to the aesthetic theory. As we have seen, process thinkers envisage all beings (from God to the lowest levels of sub-atomic life) as composed of actual entities which continually synthesize the causal data which affect them into new unities, new experiences. What is of interest to us at this point is the process thinkers' contention that this creative synthesis is motivated by an incessant and necessary quest for aesthetic value. Every new synthesis attains at least some minimal value, since with every new concrescence the "many" of the causal data become a new and unified experience. "Creativity guarantees a minimum of value to every actuality."[54] Indeed, even in the lowest levels of being where the mental poles of the constituent actual entities are underdeveloped and have not achieved consciousness, the past patterns of their beings (their physical structures) do not merely repeat themselves exactly as they were. There is always some degree of spontaneity and value, though often it is quite small and insignificant.

The aesthetic value which every concrescence seeks is that which contains an intensity and diversity amid stability, or, in other words, "a balance of unity and variety,"[55] a "harmony in diversity."[56] At every level of existence there is an appropriate degree of aesthetic value to be sought and attained. No "actuality could not not have value,"[57] since every experience is an aesthetic achievement.[58] Process thought insists that this quest for aesthetic value requires that experience contains elements not merely of order (regularity, predictability, uniformity), but also of discord and diversity. It is a mistake to equate "the good" merely with an absolute order, or lack of discord. Absolute order is as much a threat to aesthetic value as is absolute discord and chaos. The quest for experiences which are valuable requires that we escape both extremes:

> Discord, diversity not integrated by unifying factors, is not very good; but a too tame harmony or unity, not sufficiently diversified with contrasting aspects, is not very good either. And at the extreme limit, one form of aesthetic failure is as bad as the other; for in either case experience becomes impossible.[59]

Playing a scale up and down the octave, for example, "gives definite order, but not much of a melody. The orderliness is too great, too restrictive of freedom."[60] Too little order in the merely random playing of notes is also far removed from significant aesthetic value.

But it is not only the mean between too much order and too much discord which is the aesthetic ideal. Also to be sought is the mean between too much complexity and too much simplicity. The overly profound experience has little value, and there is equally little value in the overly superficial, ultra-simple, or insignificant experience.[61] An experience which escapes the extremes of absolute order and absolute disorder can still be lacking in complexity, as, for example, a single musical chord of faint musical

sounds.[62] An experience can also be barely comprehensible
in its complexity and intensity; for example, a great
climax of a symphony.[63]

EVIL AND AESTHETIC VALUE

The implications of all of this for the theodicy issue
can be readily stated. The process thinkers' main
contention is that it is mistaken, indeed profoundly
mistaken, to think that only an orderly utopia, one in
which evil and suffering do not exist (or perhaps a utopia
in which any unnecessary or avoidable evil and suffering do
not exist) is consistent with the reality of an
omnibenevolent and omnipotent God. A world of absolute
order would be one with little freedom, and it would
certainly not be populated with "creatures" (for to be a
creature is to have some degree of creativity, with its
attendant discord). God's purpose for his creatures is
that we seek experiences which avoid not only absolute
order (regularity, predictability), but also too much
discord, too much complexity and too much superficiality
(triviality). For each level of being "there is a balance
of unity and diversity which is ideally satisfying,"[64]
though, to be sure, the lower levels of existence require
and achieve far less aesthetic value than do human beings.
In rocks, for example, the aesthetic value surely is
minimal; and yet as the level of consciousness and freedom
in creatures rises, the possibilities and needs for greater
values (greater intensity and diversity) also rises.
Hartshorne often explains this in terms of the quantity of
data experienced by different levels of being:

> An electron is a principle of unity-in-contrast
> on a very small scale, or over a negligible
> portion of space. An atom is a unification of

greater contrasts, covering a larger area. A man
is the unity of the region occupied by his body.
Thus the higher types of being integrate more of
the variety of the world.[65]

Hartshorne, furthermore, has documented in great
detail the quest for aesthetic value in birds,[66] showing
that they exhibit a "[t]heme with variations" in their
singing.[67] The great majority of birds conform to the
"anti-monotony principle;" that is, they "avoid crossing
the 'monotony threshold,'" doing so by limiting the
predictability of their songs.[68] And it is likewise with
animals. All animals seek aesthetic value, and when this
is denied, lethargy sets in. A newly caged wild animal may
first experience great discord and may seek to escape, but
eventually resigned boredom will set in, and the animal's
aesthetic value will be severely limited. It is the same
with old animals: the young find life diverse and
exciting, but the old seem to retire from it in boredom.[69]

To achieve aesthetic value, variety and intensity are
required. And yet the more variety and intensity that is
experienced, the greater are the possibilities not only for
greater value and aesthetic harmony, but also for greater
risks of discord and suffering (for the data to be
synthesized is greater). "To escape triviality necessarily
means to risk discord."[70] With each new stage in the
evolution of life, from the primordial chaos to the
emergence of human beings, more and more aesthetic value
was required and achieved; and yet so too was the risk of
more and more discord. The primordial chaos contained
actual entities which existed without ordered groupings (or
"societies"). Their aesthetic value, accordingly, was
extremely trivial. "In proportion to the chaos there
[was] . . . triviality."[71] To overcome this triviality,

God lured the chaos into a more ordered state, an ordering which proceeds continually as newer and more developed and complex stages evolve. Whitehead, accordingly, informs us that "God's purpose in the creative advance is the evocation of intensities."[72] "The ultimate creative purpose [is] that each unification shall achieve some maximum depth of intensity of feeling, subject to the conditions of its concrescence."[73] The primitive chaos of unordered actual entities took on some order as "enduring individuals" were formed, that is, entities which repeated themselves (their physical patterns) through a time-sequence (protons, neutrons, electrons, etc.). And from these, more sophisticated life-forms slowly emerged: atoms, molecules, cells, and so on, with each new level of complexity representing more order and a correspondingly higher degree of aesthetic achievement. Each level is able to synthesize a greater range of data into its experience, thereby making more and more intense harmony possible. With the development of human beings, consciousness arose, making possible immensely intense and diversified experiences, for the mental poles which have developed in human beings are able, consciously, to seek novelty, rather than merely repeat past values with little variation. Human beings, however, can appropriate an immense range of possibilities either harmoniously or destructively. We are able to accept or reject the divine lure which seeks to persuade us to actualize those possibilities which will produce for us the maximum harmony. The risk of evil, consequently, is great. There is great risk not only of deliberate moral evil, but also of evils which arise unintentionally. Our freedom, then, necessarily results in some degree of conflict and suffering, for every choice of possibilities causes repercussions in the web of life around us. Without an absolute divine determinism of events, both unavoidable and deliberate evils are bound to occur.[74]

Hartshorne's "principle of positive incompatibility" is applicable here.[75] Aesthetic discord, he contends, is not necessarily or essentially a clash between goods and evils, but rather between two or more goods. Berdyaev and Whitehead saw this as well, that is, that the "conflict of positive values is at the root of both contingency and tragedy in existence. Between positive values there can be no necessary or uniquely right choice. And always some goods must be renounced."[76] Whitehead speaks of this as the evil of "loss:" with every new experience, certain values are actualized, but other potential values are not chosen, and thus lost, values which may have contributed equal (or greater) aesthetic harmony and intensity. Like Whitehead, Hartshorne locates the "ultimate reason for suffering in the world" in this principle (of positive incompatibility), together with the universal creativity of creatures.[77] "Freedom and the incompatibility of goods are enough to make a purely harmonious world impossible."[78] And yet this is a risk God is willing to take since the risk of greater evils is accompanied by the opportunities for greater aesthetic goods, goods which are necessary as life evolves toward more and more complex stages. "The freedom to enjoy a wide variety of bodily, moral and religious values intensely is also the freedom to make ourselves miserable."[79]

A WORLD WITH LESS EVIL?

A question was raised in the preceding chapter which may now be addressed in light of the present discussion of

aesthetic value. If God really is all-good and
all-powerful, should he not have created a world order in
which there is less potential for evil, less discord, less
suffering, and so on? Any world, to be sure, must have
natural laws by which it is ordered, but must these laws be
as they are, that is, such that evil and discord are so
devastatingly prevalent? "Could not an infinitely wise and
powerful God have created a world with an entirely
different structure, one in which achievement would not be
so costly? . . . . could not God have contrived a kind of
world in which life would not confront such pervasive
threats of tragedy--one possessing only positive
potentialities?"[80] The question might be reworded:
"should not God have abstained from creating a world, at
least one in which the more intense forms of evil are
possible?"[81]

From the perspective of the aesthetic theory, the
response of process thinkers seems clear: too little
complexity and intensity in our experiences (that is,
unnecessary triviality) is as much an evil to be avoided as
too little order. Discord is not the sole evil. In luring
the primordial chaos into ever greater levels of complexity
and order, accordingly, God surely is seeking to bring into
existence (for his value and for his creatures' value)
experiences which are intense and which escape unnecessary
triviality. The only way in which evil and suffering could
not have been brought into existence would have been for
God not to have stimulated the primordial chaos into more
complex and intense forms. Yet it would have been a great
evil in itself not to have done so! Since greater value
was possible, not to have lured it into a more significant
level of existence would have left the primordial chaos in
a state of unnecessary triviality. Each new step in the

evolution of beings into more complex life forms, however, brings with it new possibilities also of greater discord. In stimulating more complexity and thereby more intense forms of experience, God risks the possibilities of more intense diversity and discord; but the divine lure toward intensity and complexity also makes possible the enjoyment of the more valuable aesthetic harmonies.[82] The issue here, it seems to me, is this: should God have avoided all the goods which evolution has produced for the sake of avoiding the evils which have been produced?; "should God, for the sake of avoiding 'man's inhumanity to man,' have avoided humanity (or some comparably complex species) altogether?" To this fundamentally important question, Griffin has replied: "only those who could sincerely answer this question affirmatively would indict the God of process theology on the basis of the evil in the world."[83] In this, I believe he is correct.

Griffin adds a further point to this discussion; namely, that from the perspective of process thought, the evil which arises in the world is made more palatable by the very fact that we are not alone in suffering it. God is not an impassive absolute who merely views our suffering without concern. He is, rather, a sympathetic participant in the world, and this fact, as Griffin contends, "not only removes the basis for that sense of moral outrage which would be directed toward an impassive spectator deity who took great risks with the creation," but it also gives us some assurance that the risks are worth the taking.[84] (We feel in our own experience, moreover, that the risks are indeed worth it, for we seek intense experiences and not just those which are secure and orderly). To conceive of God as willing to suffer the evils which are by-products of new levels of complexity is reassuring. For "the one

being who is in position to know experientially the bitter
as well as the sweet fruits of the risk of creation is the
same being who has encouraged and continues to encourage
this process of creative risk-taking."[85]

THE AESTHETIC THEORY IN TRADITIONAL AND PROCESS THOUGHT

It would seem useful at this point to note how the
traditional use of the aesthetic theory differs from the
usage of aesthetic considerations in process theodicy, and
to explore some of the implications of this difference.
The traditional aesthetic theory, as noted earlier, implies
that evils are not really evils since they are, in fact,
either necessary parts of a good whole or necessary means
to a good end. The further assumption is that God permits
(or perhaps even directly causes) evils for these reasons.
The evil and suffering which arises from cancer or some
other devastating illness, for example, may have been
necessary in order to bring about the good end of tolerance
and sympathy in the sufferer or in others, and, hence, the
evil was a necessary means to the good end desired by God.
Equally so, some terrible illness may, from the divine
perspective, be merely part of a good whole; the evil,
therefore, being a necessity for the whole to be good (and
perfect, as Augustine would have it). The evil may seem to
us, from our limited and finite perspective, to be nothing
but evil; but from the perspective of the divine perfection
it is seen in its true light, as necessary for the overall
good.

From the perspective of process thought, this aspect
of the traditional theodicy is highly contentious. For one
thing, it implies an unacceptable conception of God as
either permitting (when he could have prevented it) or
directly causing evil for such reasons; and, as was argued

above, this interpretation of divine power effectively negates creaturely autonomy. It was noted, furthermore, that any divine intervention not only would appear arbitrary to us, but would undermine the necessary stability of the physical laws of nature. And it also was argued that the notion of God as deliberately causing evil (or permitting it when it could have been prevented) is inconsistent with divine goodness.

The aesthetic theory in process theodicy is markedly different from the traditional aesthetic theory. Not only does God not deliberately will certain evils for aesthetic ends, but the evils and sufferings of the world's creatures are seen as evils--and not merely as apparent evils which are necessary for good ends or for the overall good. Process theodicy, nevertheless, contends that the evils of the world are, in an important sense, "overcome" by God. This implies, in Hartshorne's words, that "deity realizes the most good which can be achieved through synthesis into new subjective forms, which include the evil to be sure, but much more besides."[86] Evil is not obliterated in God's experience of the world's evil or seen as something other than it is, but rather becomes part of his everlasting experience. Yet "not the evil alone, rather the evil with or in its ideal complement of vision."[87] Evils are not omitted or negated, according to Hartshorne, but rather, "God adds to all such evils a context which produces in relation to them, whatever good can be made to result."[88] God's experience of evil is supplemented by his perfect retention of all past values, so that his experience is always "a net increment of value,"[89] a surplus of value: "the fact that God inherits all our feelings does not mean that he is in danger of finding

disvalue overbalancing value. Even for us this does not
occur" since there is always value in every experience. If
experience had less than a net increment of value it could
not continue. Every "experience as a whole is a value
rather than a disvalue . . . . We wring some kind of
satisfaction, however poor or strained, out of pain and
frustration; though we may feel very keenly how much better
life might be."[90]   Evils are not negated by God's
experience of them, but rather they are harmonized into a
greater synthesis wherein all past goods are fully
experienced together with all the good which lies
potentially within the evil; "partly evil occurrences are
changed from isolated entities by being taken into a new
whole of ideal sympathy and vision beholding also what the
future can best do with the good and the evil in them."[91]

     At this point, however, I would raise the question:
is it true that our experience always contains a net
increment of value? Indeed, does God's experience of the
world always contain more value then disvalue? It is one
thing to argue that every experience has at least minimal
value but another to contend that this value always
contains a surplus of good over evil. The fact that we go
on living testifies to the fact that there is value in our
experiences, for without this value there would be no
stimulus for further living: "[w]hen life offers us less
than nothing, we do not live."[92]   And this, to be sure,
is the basis of Hartshorne's rejection of the contention
that some evil is merely gratuitous.[93]   But Hartshorne
insists that there is not just value but a net increment of
value, and that it is this surplus to which is attributed
the stimulus to seek further experiences. In reference to
creatures he acts rhetorically: "if life were not more
satisfying than otherwise, could it go on?"[94]   And in

reference to God he insists that "the total character of God's life" is always "overwhelmingly joyous," though he adds here that the life of creatures "is not always" joyous.[95] Without this qualification it seems to me that Hartshorne would be seeking to establish too much. Is it not enough that every experience achieves some value? Why must there be a surplus of value? I can appreciate somewhat his point in reference to God's experience, for the world as a whole (the object of God's experience) must perhaps have more order than disorder; otherwise, it could not function as a world order. Yet, perhaps God's experience of the great human anguish within this world order is not one of great joy. The immense amount of anguish and suffering of the creatures (human and non-human) seems overwhelming, despite the fact that there is some value in every experience. Rather than arguing that there is a surplus of good in God's experience and in (a great many of) the experiences of human beings, would it not, then, be better simply to argue that there is at least some value in every experience? There are a "few human beings, to be sure, who seem to be overcome by overwhelmingly negative experiences, but even for those who suffer anguish to such an extent that life seems meaningless to them, the will to live is often sustained, conceivably, by faith and hope for future good (and this need not necessarily be in reference to some post mortem world). Any value we have experienced in the past, despite our suffering, and any value we may hope for in the future would seem to offer a sufficient stimulus (in most cases) to continue our striving in the creative advance for aesthetic achievement.

EVIL "OVERCOME" BY GOD

But let us turn now to a question which has arisen more specifically in reference to the process thinkers' contention that God "overcomes" evil. Some critics insist that the overcoming of evil in no way benefits the creatures who have suffered the evil and, accordingly, the God who overcomes it in his own experience is hardly benevolent. The evil, it is argued, serves merely to intensify the overall harmony of God's experience. Ely, for example, contends that creaturely experiences (goods and evils) are not really valued by God for their own sakes, but rather serve merely as the "instruments of God's [aesthetic] joy."[96] God may see the evil in its full value, yet for us it "is not help for [our] present ills to know that God sees them in such a way that they are valuable for him."[97]

Hartshorne, however, has responded to this critique, pointing out, first of all, that for God altruism and self-interest are perfectly coincidental. God's altruism toward his creatures constitutes his own self-interest "without being any the less altruism."[98] Indeed, "[t]o expect God not to benefit by any benefits he bestows is to deny his omniscience; or it is to claim that a loving being could fully know the joy he produces in others and remain unpleased by this as well as untroubled by their sufferings."[99] While human knowledge of things in the world is always partial and inadequate, for God, however, all things are internal and immediate because he experiences them fully and completely. Hartshorne insists that "only a mere machine that blindly passed out benefits could conform to the notion of a benevolence that had nothing to gain from the success of its services to others."[100]

There is a second aspect of process theodicy which can be utilized in direct response to Ely's critique. The evils experienced and "overcome" by God do <u>not</u> merely remain part of the divine experience but, in fact, are <u>passed</u> <u>back</u> into the world for the benefit of its creatures! The harmony experienced by God becomes a "particular providence for particular occasions."[101] Griffin has addressed this point as it is presented in Whitehead's thought, explaining that God overcomes evil in the sense that "in responding to the evil facts in the world, [he] provides ideal aims for the next state of the world designed to overcome the evil in the world."[102] In constantly luring creatures toward ideal aims, God takes into account all the goods and evils that already have been actualized by creatures. His synthetic experience appreciates whatever goods are possible next, and this divine perception becomes the creaturely "initial aim:" "the perfected actuality passes back into the temporal world, and qualifies this world so that each temporal actuality includes it as an immediate fact of relevant experience . . . . What is done in the world is transformed into a reality in heaven [that is, in God's experience] and the reality in heaven passes back into the world."[103] In part, the divine lure is apprehended as a moral impetus for us to enact good ends. In this way, God's overcoming of evil in the world surely is actively felt.[104]

In order to overcome evils, God must, of course, first experience them. But the criticism might be raised here that if God experiences evils as well as goods, <u>he himself</u> must be both evil and good. Hartshorne (with Berdyaev, Whitehead and others) does believe that in experiencing the world's evil, God, in fact, does <u>suffer</u> our evil: God is

that "being to whom suffering is never alien,"[105] who
"sorrows in all our sorrows,"[106] who is the "cosmic
sufferer, who endures infinitely more evil than we can
imagine."[107] He is, in Whitehead's classic phrase, "the
great companion--the fellow sufferer who understands."[108]
This point is itself contentious, for many would hold that
a God who suffers is less than the God of absolute
perfection demanded by religious faith. Is not such
perfection supposedly beyond suffering? And yet it is
essential to the process position that God _is_ affected by
the world, that his perfection lies not in his independence
of and immunity to the world, but in his perfect response
to the world's contingent acts and decisions. The fact
that God _experiences_ the world's evil, moreover, does not
make God himself evil; for it is one thing for him to
experience the evil committed by another, and quite a
different thing to _be_ evil himself. "God feels wicked
feelings not as his own feelings but as his
creatures'."[109] This is consistent with the Whiteheadian
category of "feeling of feeling," which implies a
subject-object duality:

> The first feeling [God's] is the "subjective
> form" of the experience, the second [the
> creatures'] the "objective form." Both are
> feelings, but the second is the original (and
> temporally prior), the first is a participation
> in the second after the fact. Wickedness is in
> wrong decisions. God inherits our decisions, as
> ours, not as his. In feeling them he does not
> enact or decide them; for they are already
> decided.[110]

God's experiences, like the experiences of all beings,
produce a new harmony, a new "one" from the "many" elements

of the data experienced. "The 'harmony' effected is not in the data as prehended (as objective data) but in the rightness of feeling with which God shapes his own ("universal") subjective forms, his feelings about our feelings, not our feelings simply as participated in by him, as 'objective forms' of feeling."[111] "The more can contain the less;" God is more than the world and its actualized values. He is constituted not solely by his response to the world but also by his response to his own antecedent responses, so that while he is affected by the world, he transcends the world.[112] "The most wicked act," accordingly, "is literally in God, and while wicked as our volition, as divine impulse it is not subject to ethical description, positive or negative."[113]

THE QUESTION OF IMMORTALITY

There is a final issue to be considered, one which has become in the minds of many scholars a major point of contention with process thought. These critics find inadequate the process view which postulates that there is no final good to be achieved, no final end of the processive sequence of events wherein the entire creation (or parts of it) will be brought to a good and perfect fruition (as, for example, Teilhard's "Omega Point," the "Parousia," or, simply, Heaven, where suffering and toil will be no more and where all will be fulfilled.) Process thought--at least as it is represented by Whitehead, Hartshorne, and most of their followers--claims that there is no personal immortality in the traditional sense, no heavenly realm of blissful joy and eternal peace.[114] The process view is that our immortality is in fact to live forever in the mind of God, not consciously as we now live, but rather as data in the eternal divine experience.

Critics protest that such a view not only deindividualizes us, but is inadequate as a Christian position, or, indeed, from any truly theistic perspective. Many would argue, with John Hick, moreover, that unless there is an afterlife existence for human beings, the theodicy question is finally unresolved and unresolvable. "Would it not contradict God's love for the creatures made in His image if He caused them to pass out of existence whilst His purpose for them was still so largely unfulfilled?"[115] Unless all the evil and suffering undergone by human beings is redeemed, Hick contends, God "is not perfect in love or He is not sovereign in rule over His creation."[116]

From the perspective of process thought, however, the requirement that there be an afterlife existence is not only unnecessary but is in fact not essential to Christianity or to a resolution of the theodicy issue. There is, of course, a strong sentimental appeal in the idea that our sufferings will be redeemed, and that we shall meet our friends and loved ones in the afterlife. There is an even stronger egotistical desire that we ourselves shall live forever.[117] But the process position is that an afterlife existence of this sort is not essential to Christianity; what is essential is the assurance that our existence on earth has some ultimate value and meaning. The chief need for immortality, according to Hartshorne, is not an escape from bodily dissolution, but a need for permanence; and the "basic question of permanence concerns not so much the perished men as the perished states or experiences of men."[118] Indeed, "unless our joys and sorrows in some way enrich the universe throughout all future time," they are merely "passing whiffs of insignificance;"[119] life would be the absurd production of values "only to cast them on the rubbish heap as fast as they are there."[120] In place of a personal immortality wherein human beings would live everlastingly as conscious, active subjects, Hartshorne and other process thinkers find more viable the Whiteheadian notion of "objective immortality:" all finite reality is forever retained in the experience of God; all creatures are immortalized in God as data or objects of his eternal and perfect awareness. Objective immortality alone secures our true immortality, the permanence of all we have experienced and achieved. The alternatives of "social" and "personal" immortality are clearly less adequate.

Social immortality locates the ultimate meaning and value of our lives in the memories of creaturely posterity. Yet this surely fails to secure the permanence of values. It is possible (indeed, probable) that our race will eventually become extinct and, in this event, all of our experiences will be lost forever. And even if our race were to survive, social immortality would still be an inadequate basis for the immortality of values, since neither our contemporaries nor posterity will know or remember much about any of us, save perhaps the lives of a few famous people.[121] Human memory is clearly deficient, and there is need, accordingly, for "an individual who is not subject to the incurable ignorance of human perception, understanding, and memory."[122] This individual, of course, is God, and it is Hartshorne's contention that "if deity cannot furnish the abiding reality of events, there is . . . no other way, intelligible to us at least, in which it can be furnished."[123]

But what of personal immortality? Would not the eternal existence of human beings in some post mortem realm render everlastingly meaningful the entire sequence of experiences and acts which constitute our individual

lives? Hartshorne's position is that it would not. The
basic question concerning the ultimate meaning of our
experiences is not to be found in the immortality of human
beings but in the immortality of our past lives, exactly
and fully as they occurred. "Without the immortality of
experiences, any heaven would," Hartshorne insists,
"present the same problem of the transience of
experiences."[124] Eternal life in heaven would involve
the accumulation of an infinity of new experiences; but
this would do little to guarantee the permanence of our
past experiences. For unless we are to become beings
significantly other than we are now, it is difficult to
imagine that we would be any more capable than we are now
of remembering fully our past lives. And indeed if we were
to become other than we are now, it would be highly
unlikely that we could be called the same self-identical
persons.[125] "In unlimited future time, unlimited novelty
must accrue (unless there is to be ever increasing monotony
or boredom), and yet one is [on the traditional view of
personal immortality] to be oneself, just that individual
and no other, and not identical with God."[126]
Hartshorne's contention, to the contrary, is that "[i]f our
capacity to assimilate new future content and yet remain
ourselves . . . is unlimited, then in that respect we are
exactly as God is."[127] But it is a characteristic of God
alone to be capable of eternally assimilating novelty and
yet to remain self-identical. If we human beings are what
we are, and not God, then we are "limited, a fragment of
reality, not the whole."[128] It is surely a truism that
as creatures, we are spatially and temporally limited, that
we are parts of the whole, and that our very reality is
defined by such limitations.[129] We must, as Hartshorne
insists, be aware that it is not our deaths which would

make life absurd and meaningless, but _God's_, though the
latter possibility is itself absurd, for God's existence
(for Hartshorne, at any rate) is by definition a
necessity.[130]

Hartshorne is aware that in denying a continuing
personal immortality, his alternative position will seem
unacceptable to many people within a religious tradition
which has almost unanimously postulated subjective
immortality as an essential and central aspect of its
faith. Does not a mere objective immortality destroy any
chance to make amends for the errors we have committed in
this life? Does it not deny us the opportunity to grow
deeper in insight and devotion beyond the grave? Does it
not deny us compensation for the earthly suffering and
injustice we have endured? Hartshorne's response to such
concerns is that they are based on confusing individual
self-interest with the good of the whole.[131] Is it not
enough, he asks, that our lives contribute to God's
experience and to other beings? Must we ourselves live on
beyond the grave to acquire a state of absolute good? "He
who says that belief in the divine enjoyment of a richer
life than ours, to which our own can contribute, and which
in turn will contribute to the lives of creatures yet to
come, can be no consolation to us for the trials of
existence is simply denying that we can genuinely love
either God or man."[132] The traditional Christian
conception of immortality, of an afterlife in heaven (or in
hell), Hartshorne believes, is largely the result of the
concept of personal substance and our enshrinement of
self-interest as ultimate.[133] We have maintained a
"secret egotism"[134] that we ourselves shall live on,
consciously, forever, that we shall "enjoy divine
privileges, not just our own human ones;" indeed, "we have

regarded God, not as the end of ends, but as means to our own end, the achievement of permanence!"[135] "All good," however, as Hartshorne insists, "cannot be my good; only God is heir to all good."[136]

Arguments, furthermore, that personal immortality is essential to compensate (reward or punish) earthly life seem especially irrational to Hartshorne. Human beings are constituted by some necessary degree of autonomy in respect to our acts and decisions, and accordingly, there is not a divine determinism but an element of chance involved in the goods we experience. The same is true for the suffering and conflicts we must endure: "if each particular entity is selfdetermining, how can there be harmony between the entities?"[137] God determines only the general limits to our freedom, limits within which we can act; he does not determine the details of our acts and decisions, though he continually persuades and lures us to actualize those values which will contribute both to ourselves and others the most intensity and harmoniously significant experiences which are possible.[138] Hartshorne contends, accordingly, that any heaven, populated by human beings, must be subject to the same risks of freedom which are operative in this life. It is difficult to see, then, how heaven can be a place of compensatory rewards and punishments imposed by God. Goods and evils will continue not to be in exact proportion to our past deeds, for "where there is chance there will be 'injustice.'"[139] The traditional theory of heavenly compensation, accordingly, "seems incompatible with the nature of existence."[140] It is, of course, not the case that God is unjust, but rather that "He is not engaged in rewarding or punishing in this bookkeeping sense at all."[141] God's role is not to manipulate events but to ensure that there are opportunities for free, creative acts decided by human beings (and proportionately by lesser levels of beings).[142]   Hartshorne rejects the "transcendental hedonism" (Paley) of the traditional view, and cites approvingly Berdyaev's designation of it as "the most disgusting morality ever conceived."[143]   "God does not stamp on the bodies or the souls who have lived ill; nor does He insult those who found love its own reward with post mortem rewards so out of proportion to all the goods of this life that a reasonable man could think of nothing else if he really took them seriously."[144]   God is neither sadistic nor vengeful, Hartshorne insists, and the "attempt to combine such things with divine mercy should be given up."[145]   Our reward and punishment for our acts and decisions is now, in the aesthetic value (the intensity and harmony of experience) we achieve.   Our only future compensation is that we contribute to other beings and to God.   The "divine judgment" of our lives is that our acts and experiences are final, and eternally present to God as such.[146]   We can make our lives a "reasonable, holy, and living sacrifice" to God,[147] or we can contribute far less than we are, in fact, able to.   In either case, we have our reward or punishment in the immediate experience.

Let us note, however, that it is not the case that we are to act lovingly and seek the fullest good which is possible at each moment merely as means whereby God achieves his own ends.   Rather, what God seeks and enjoys is our enjoyment.   We enjoy the beauty and harmony of the world, to be sure, in a fragmentary way, while God enjoys the full value of the entire world in his perfect vision.[148]   We do, nevertheless, contribute value to God; his experience of the world includes its diversity and also its ugliness and discord.   His experience includes, furthermore, the world's overall unity and beauty.   "God knows the world as a whole, and therefore knows its ultimate harmony in spite of its obvious discord . . . . without God there would be no enjoyment of the integral beauty." It would be wasted "and rendered meaningless."[149] God, then, secures our acts as everlastingly meaningful and we in turn contribute to his own aesthetic experience. This is the "significance of man" and "the purpose of the universe."[150]

Some critics argue, however, that God's love for us conceivably would not permit death to destroy us, and hence that we must live on subjectively. But Hartshorne's response is to point out emphatically that death does not constitute our sheer destruction.[151] Death terminates our conscious sequence of acts and experiences, to be sure, yet all that we have experienced and accomplished can never die, since our full reality is retained perfectly and eternally in God. God's love for us is not measured by the granting of personal immortality but by the fact that his eternal experience of our full reality gives our acts and experiences everlasting value and meaning. "The true immortality is everlasting fame before God."[152] God, after all, created us as finite creatures, and if he could not "suffer us to be limited, then He . . . [could not] suffer us to be at all, as limited creatures or as other than Himself."[153]

There is a further argument to be considered, nevertheless, the "best argument for personal survival in the conventional sense:"[154] since life is cumulative and many potentialities are lost when a human being dies, is it not wasteful for life always to begin over again with new individuals? Hartshorne's response, however, is to point out the fundamental aesthetic principle that while life is cumulative, "it is just as true that it is self-exhaustive."[155] No life other than God's can accommodate an infinite variety of experiences which maintain the intensity and novelty required to make them aesthetically significant and valuable.[156] "Each of us is a theme with variations," a finite number of variations, and "it is better to turn to a new art form [a new life] than to exhaust possible variations on the old."[157] Premature death, to be sure, is unquestionably a great tragedy, for it cuts off potentially significant experiences; yet premature death is brought about by chance, not by divine providence.[158] Death itself is not tragic, since it "is only a boundary, establishing the definiteness, the distinctiveness, of each non-divine theme."[159] Human life is a series of stages: infancy, childhood, adolescence, the prime of life, and old age. Each stage provides fresh and novel possibilities which can be experienced, and each stage "lasts long enough so the variations on the theme of the stage in question are not tediously numerous, yet numerous enough to bring out the value of the themes . . . . A theme is worth a finite, not an infinite number of variations."[160] God, however, in experiencing what is concretely new each moment, "must reform His awareness of us forever, so that we function as a theme for eternally endless variations in the use God makes of us as objects of His awareness to be synthesized with ever additional objects."[161] It is not our privilege to live on subjectively as God does, and yet "we may earn everlasting places as lives well lived within the one life that not only evermore will have been lived, but evermore and inexhaustibly will be lived in ever new ways."[162]

Hartshorne has also responded to the criticism that objective immortality is an unacceptable alternative to the traditional view of immortality in as much as it implies that, in making our lives part of his own, God deindividualizes us. "God could not," it is argued, "merge me and my values into an indefinitely immense system and still claim that I have maintained my individuality and my values;"[163] "my achieved individual values may be eternally the means, immortally contemplated by God, but he sees them as part of a system. Their individuality, even for God, has perished."[164] Hartshorne's response is that this criticism virtually ignores (or rejects without argument) Whitehead's fundamental insight that actualities can be experienced (prehended) by other actualities and yet retain their individuality. It is true that we who are not God must "abstract" somewhat in prehending other finite realities, yet God prehends all things "without loss of immediacy" and excludes nothing.[165]

Hartshorne insists, furthermore, that since objective immortality in God eternally and fully retains all we have ever experienced and done, this in fact is a "personal immortality" in a most significant sense. "If one's actual concrete experiences are not personal," he argues, "I do not know what would be. They represent all that one actually is . . . . Those who want to 'wake up' in heaven are not asking for the preservation of their earthly actuality; rather they ask for the actualization of additional possibilities."[166] It is, of course, this distinction upon which the process view centers: immortality is the preservation of the already actualized experiences, not the opportunity for endless further experiences.[167] And, as noted earlier, Hartshorne believes that the "preservation of what we create in ourselves and others suffices to give life a lasting meaning;" on the other hand, "to ask also for endless further self-creation is not easily distinguishable from asking that we should be God, who indeed is endlessly self-creative."[168]

If, finally, we were to question the adequacy of the process thinkers' view that making service to God the ultimate purpose of our lives is a viable and meaningful religious goal, Hartshorne's position is that it is, and that we do so because of God's love: "Why ask for a motive for loving God, and for making service to Him the ultimate end? Either the motive for loving God is His lovableness, or it is something else. If it is His lovableness, then that is sufficient . . . . If the motive must be something else, then God is deficiently lovable, which is blasphemous."[169]

In sum, there is in process theodicy no ultimate or final good that creation as such will achieve, other than being eternally and fully remembered in God's experience. There is no final heavenly state populated by experiencing, conscious subjects. But the ultimate question of the permanence of our values has been answered, and this is really what is essential to the religious life. That we might live on consciously "seems at best a secondary matter, a problematic luxury."[170]

Chapter 10: CONCLUSION

Process theodicy, as we have just seen, does not support the traditional view that present evils and suffering will somehow be compensated in an afterlife existence. Nor does it espouse the view that human beings will be brought to a final and perfect fruition. There is no "redemption" in this sense, despite those who insist that a final and perfect completion of every individual human life is essential.[171] Hartshorne's argument is that what really is essential is the assurance that our earthly acts and decisions have everlasting value and meaning, and this is to be attained not by an infinity of new acts and decisions in a post mortem world or by reaching a state of ultimate fulfillment, but by our past lives being fully and perfectly experienced by God. And just as God does not directly cause the evil and suffering we endure or directly intervene intermittently to prevent or eradicate certain specific evils, neither does he directly compensate us for such suffering, nor bring us to a final and perfect state. The evil and suffering we have endured are to be attributed to the free creativity of all creatures and to by-products of the natural laws which support creaturely life. God's role is to persuasively guide his creatures to experience those values and goods which are the best possible in every situation and to appropriate our experiences as part of his own everlasting reality. To demand or expect a continuing, unending opportunity for subjective experiences after death is an understandable but essentially misdirected hope. It is not the case that a loving God would necessarily grant us such an opportunity.

For some, these proposals may be far from comforting, yet process thinkers have good reasons for rejecting the alternative traditional beliefs. Belief, for example, in a realm of everlasting subjective experiences may be emotionally appealing to most of us, but it is not without rational difficulties, as Hartshorne has shown. It cannot, moreover, legitimately be used as a solution to the theodicy issue; it cannot make right the injustices of this life, nor indeed is it even essential in establishing what it seeks to establish: the permanence of our experiences and values. It is God's everlasting experience of our earthly careers which alone guarantees such permanence.

The traditional belief, furthermore, that God is actually or potentially in control of worldly affairs is certainly far more reassuring than the view of process thinkers that the divine causal agency operates solely as a lure to persuade creatures toward the best ends possible at each moment. But a coercive God who either controls all things directly or intervenes intermittently is hardly a God who could permit significant or consistently meaningful creaturely freedom. Such a conception of divine power is, as Hartshorne has long contended, a pseudoconcept which pays an unnecessary metaphysical compliment to God. It simply is _not_ the case that God, as God, must potentially or actually have controlling power.

The fact that traditional theology by and large has missed this point has contributed to the perplexity of the theodicy issue. Hartshorne is hardly exaggerating in his condemnation of the traditional view as "but a mass of undigested notions too vague or self-inconsistent to permit any useful application to rational argument."[172] For despite insisting that human beings are free and morally responsible agents, traditional theology conceives God as literally "all-powerful", implying thereby that the world's evils as well as its goods are somehow in accord with his will and purpose. This view, held ultimately as a mystery of faith, has resulted in various explanations for evil which either deny its reality (since as God's will, evil must really be a good in disguise which serves some unknown and unknowable divine function), or in explanations which attribute the world's evil to divine punishments, tests, or warnings and the like. From the perspective of process theodicy, however, such attempts to account for evil are regarded as thoroughly misguided and problematic. Among other things, they render such horrors as birth defects and serious childhood anguish and disease as somehow in accord with God's will and plan, a conclusion which cannot be softened or made more palatable by attributing the evil to human free will (for the traditional conception of God virtually negates free will in creatures) or by appealing to the dubious doctrine of original sin. Serious questions surely must be raised as to why a God who supposedly controls all events--or at least has the power to do so--has caused or permitted so much destruction and anguish. It is hardly justifiable or reasonable to attribute such evil to Satan and his cohorts, or to appeal to a heavenly compensation which will somehow make things right. Yet "out of such stuff has the problem of evil been generated,"[173] and one can only empathize with innumerable generations of sufferers whose faith in God has been put to the test unfairly by the belief that God himself is responsible for their anguish. It is clear, to process thinkers at least, why so many people, in the face of seemingly unjustifiable suffering, have rejected belief in the God of traditional Christianity. For while it may be somehow reassuring to believe that God is in control and that his will is being done on earth, to believe that he has caused or permitted the world's great pain and anguish (and that he could have prevented it) is hardly a God who can inspire love and worship. The modern rise of atheism and spiritual despair is in part directly attributable to such a belief.

What process thinkers contribute to the theodicy question is an understanding of God which holds that he is not responsible for specific goods and evils, but only for there being real possibilities for goods and thus, unavoidably, for evils. All creatures have some degree of genuine autonomy (freedom in human beings) which God can influence only persuasively. I have argued in this book, however, that there is some question as to whether Hartshorne has adequately constructed this conception of divine persuasive power. Does God act solely persuasively or with some degree of coercive power? My contention is that in imposing the natural laws as the limits to creaturely freedom, and despite Hartshorne's protests to the contrary, his God does seem to act coercively. I have suggested, moreover, that there are good reasons in support of this argument (since, for example, it is difficult to comprehend how creatures themselves could account for such laws).[174] Yet this is hardly an issue which is settled: Hartshorne believes that the imposition of laws is a persuasive act and despite my interpretation to the contrary I am open, certainly, to this possibility. My complaint is that Hartshorne has not justified his position with convincing clarity.[175] Whitehead believed, moreover, that the natural laws are immanent rather than imposed, a view eloquently defended by Lewis Ford.[176]

Yet an even more pressing question has to do not with God's causal power with respect to the laws of nature, but with his activity in influencing creaturely acts and decisions within the limits defined by these laws. Process thinkers argue that such divine activity is solely persuasive and propose strong arguments against its being coercive. Coercive action by God would, they contend, be impossible since creatures, as such, necessarily have some degree of autonomy. Coercive action, moreover, would be arbitrary (at least to human eyes) and would seem to have no justifiable parameters until all evil was eliminated from the world. But this would jeopardize the very possibility of there being spiritually significant creatures, creatures which are free to choose or reject God's lure. Divine coercive intervention in the natural order of things, furthermore, would render unreliable (and thus meaningless and impossible) human moral values and intellectual pursuits, for these depend upon a stable world order.

But there are those who insist that some divine coercion may be both morally and religiously necessary. Gerald Janzen has made this point most strongly,[177] as has the late Daniel Day Williams.[178] My own suggestion has been that despite Hartshorne's protests that his God acts solely persuasively, much of what he says about that agency seems in fact to be more properly defined as coercive. As such, Hartshorne's God may well be more in control than it would appear. And this is the case not only with respect to the imposition of the laws of nature, but also with respect to God's inspiration of creaturely acts at every moment within those limits. Divine power, to be sure, cannot be such as to completely override creaturely autonomy, but there is surely a wide range of power, short of absolute coercion, which God can utilize.[179]   Yet precisely what this range is is by no means clear. It may be somewhat akin to the influence one person can have over another, the influence being so persuasive, in certain cases, that it is more properly referred to as coercive. There must be more involved than this simplistic suggestion; but, at any rate, my point is that in describing the divine agency as, for example, "irresistible" and "unconsciously" effective, Hartshorne does appear to give God's persuasive lure a rather coercive coloring. And yet, that agency is never so coercive as to completely override creaturely autonomy, for if this were the case (were such even possible) process theodicy would face the same perplexing and unanswerable problems which confront the traditional theodicy. Process thinkers are concerned to avoid such issues; they do not wish to have to answer the question as to why God has not intervened more often if indeed he has the coercive capability to do so. Nor do they wish to have to solve the paradox (or, rather, contradiction) as to how human beings can be genuinely free and partially autonomous subjects, morally responsible for good and evil acts, when God's power can (and apparently does) fully determine their acts and decisions. But while denying that God acts with an absolute coerciveness which would completely override creaturely autonomy, or indeed that he permits creaturely acts when he has the power to prevent them, what remains to be more clearly articulated by process thinkers is how, precisely, divine persuasive power affects creatures; that is, with what degree of persuasion and coercion. This, as I indicated above, will not be an easy task, for the precise workings of the divine causal agency may well be forever inaccessible to human comprehension. Yet there is surely some headway to be made, short of an omniscient illumination.

In conclusion, I would suggest that while the process

theodicy may not be the complete and final word on the theodicy issue,[180] its contribution to the traditional Christian problem of evil is indisputably a major achievement. The fact that the full implications of this contribution have not as yet been adequately assessed, exploited and critically refined is an unjustifiable and tragic omission, unworthy of serious theological studies. It is my modest hope that this present book has contributed somewhat to amending this situation.

NOTES

CHAPTER 1:   GOOD AND EVIL

1. While most discussions of the theodicy issue
seem to be unaware of the contribution of process thinkers,
there are a handful of notable exceptions, some of which
were mentioned in the Preface. Peter Hare and Edward
Madden, in Evil and the Concept of God (Springfield: C. C.
Thomas, 1968), propose a number of criticisms against both
traditional theodicy and process theodicy; Michael
Galligan, in God and Evil (New York: Paulist Press, 1976),
does likewise; and John Hick offers a short summary and
critique of the process position in the third edition of
his Philosophy of Religion (Englewood Cliffs: Prentice
Hall, 1983). Paul Schilling's excellent study, God and
Human Anguish (Nashville: Abingdon, 1977), makes passing
reference to process thought; and two works by process
theologians themselves deal with process theodicy: David
R. Griffin's God, Power and Evil: A Process Theodicy
(Philadelphia: Westminster, 1976), and Norman Pittenger's
Cosmic Love and Human Wrong (New York: Paulist Press,
1978). Pittenger's book is an analysis on the concept of
sin from the perspective of process thought, while
Griffin's is virtually the only major study of process
theodicy published in book form. Griffin also has a
chapter on process theodicy in Encountering Evil (Atlanta:
John Knox Press, 1981), 101-136, a text edited by Stephen
T. Davis.
    There have been a number of articles and book chapters
published which offer both critiques and sympathetic
studies of process theodicy. Hartshorne's "A New Look at
the Problem of Evil," in F. C. Dommeyer, ed., Current
Philosophical Issues: Essays in Honor of Curt John Ducasse
(Springfield: C. C. Thomas, 1966), 201-212, is the best
summary of his position, although he considers here only
part of his overall theodicy. Hartshorne has several other
references to the theodicy issue scattered unsystematically

throughout numerous other articles and book chapters. See also D. D. Baldwin's study, "Evil and Persuasive Power: A Response to Hare and Madden," Process Studies (1973), 259-272; John Cobb, God and the World (Philadelphia: Westminster, 1969), 87-102; N. Pittenger, "Process Theology and the Fact of Evil," The Expository Times (1971), 73-77; P. Hefner, "Is Theodicy a Question of Power?," Journal of Religion (1979), 87-93; D. D. Williams, "The Victory of Good," Journal of Liberal Religion (1942), 171-185; F. Wood, "Some Whiteheadian Insights into the Problem of Evil," Southwestern Journal of Philosophy (1979), 147-155; and N. Frankenberry, "Some Problems in Process Theodicy," Religious Studies (1982), 179-197.

2. See B. Brody, ed., Readings in the Philosophy of Religion (Englewood Cliffs: Prentice-Hall, 1974), 485. The passage cited is that of the little-known German idealist, Malwida von Meysenbug.

3. Hartshorne contends, I believe rightly, that religious experience is "ubiquitous," and that rather than "finding severe paradox in the idea of direct experience of deity, or the unsurpassable, it is . . . a paradox to suppose that such a reality could be known or truly affirmed only on the basis of indirect evidence" (Charles Hartshorne, "Mysticism and Rationalistic Metaphysics," Monist [1976], 463).

4. See John Cobb and David Griffin, Process Theology (Philadelphia: Westminster, 1976), 30-40.

5. R. Otto, The Idea of the Holy (London: Oxford University Press, 1923). Whitehead describes the religious experience in terms of value: we intuit that we ourselves have value, that all individuals have value for one another, and that the world has value (Religion in the Making, [New York: Macmillan, 1926], 58). The religious experience is the intuition of a "permanent rightness, whose inheritance in the nature of things modifies both efficient and final cause" (Religion in the Making, 60). For good accounts of Whitehead's understanding of religious experience see: Lawrence Wilmot, Whitehead and God (Waterloo: Wilfred Laurier University Press, 1979), 19-29; Kathleen Fischer, "Religious Experience in Lonergan and Whitehead," Religious Studies (1980), 69-79; and William O'Meara, "Whitehead's Description of Religious Intuition," Encounter (1973), 101-113.

6. See Cobb and Griffin, Process Theology, 30-40; and Hartshorne, "Mysticism," 463-469.

7. Cited in Nelson Pike, ed., God and Evil (Englewood Cliffs: Prentice-Hall, 1964), 19. The reference is from Hume's Dialogues Concerning Natural Religion.

8. Cited in Pike, God and Evil, 20.

9. George Joyce, Principles of Natural Theology (London: Longmans, Green and Company, 1923), 584, cited by H. J. McCloskey, in Pike, God and Evil, 64.

10. See, for example, Charles Hartshorne, Man's Vision of God and the Logic of Theism (Chicago: Willett, Clark and Company, 1941; reprinted by Archon Books, Hamden, Conn., 1964), 6.

11. Hick, Evil and the God of Love, (New York:Harper and Row, 1966, revised edition, 1978), 11.

12. See Schilling, God and Human Anguish, 29-49.

CHAPTER 2: THE FAITH SOLUTION

13. The phrase is Nelson Pike's. See his "Hume on Evil," in Pike, God and Evil, 88.

14. See Cobb and Griffin, Process Theology, 69.

15. See Schilling, God and Human Anguish, 60-64. Schilling offers several examples of this belief, from the Book of Job to Ann Landers. In a 1974 column, Landers expressed the opinion that things occur (in this case, a particular tragedy) because it "was God's will. He had a reason . . . . You must believe that God in his infinite wisdom had a reason—not known to you now, but it is there" (64). Examples of this attitude could be amplified almost infinitely.

16. See Schilling, God and Human Anguish, 67-72.

17. See, for example, Dom Helder Camara, Revolution Through Peace, trans., Amparo McLean, (New York: Seabury Press, 1969); D. H. Camara, The Church and Colonialism, trans., William McSweeney (Denville, N. J.: Dimension Books, 1969); James Cone, A Black Theology of Liberation (Philadelphia: J. B. Lippincott, 1970); Martin Marty and Dean Peerman, eds., New Theology, No. 6: On Revolution and Non-Revolution, Violence and Non-Violence, Peace and Power (New York: Macmillan, 1969); Alistar Kee, ed., A Reader in Political Theology (London: SCM, 1974); and from the perspective of process thought, see John Cobb, Process

Theology as Political Theology (Philadelphia: Westminster,
1982); John Cobb and W. Widick Schroeder, eds., Process
Philosophy and Social Thought (Chicago: Center for the
Scientific Study of Religion, 1981); and Schubert
Ogden, Faith and Freedom (Nashville: Abingdon, 1979).

18. Hick is probably correct in his observation that
"all theological activity is in danger of impiety," but, as
he also points out, this does not mean that all theological
thinking should cease! "By what authority," he asks, "must
we insist upon maintaining an unrelieved mystery and
darkness concerning God's permission of evil?" Despite the
fact that human reason is fallible, surely rational inquiry
about the theodicy issue (as about other beliefs: the
trinity, creation, heaven and hell, etc.) is not without
its merit: "certain approaches to it may be less
inadequate than others, and it may thus be possible to
reach some modest degree of genuine illumination upon the
subject and to discover helpful criteria by which to
discriminate among speculations concerning it" (Hick, Evil
and the God of Love, 7-8).

19. Hick, Evil and the God of Love, 210. See Hick's
account of how the "fall" story rose to prominence in the
Old Testament world and in subsequent thought (Hick, Evil
and the God of Love, 201-211).

20. There are, of course, countless creation myths
among the world's peoples and an abundance of explanations
for evil. See Barbara C. Sproul, Primal Myths (San
Francisco: Harper and Row, 1979). And John Bowker,
Problems of Suffering in Religions of the World (Cambridge:
Cambridge University Press, 1970).

21. For useful discussions of the nature of myths,
see Larry Shinn, Two Sacred Worlds (Nashville: Abingdon,
1977), 85-120; and Frederick Streng, Understanding
Religious Life (Encino and Belmont, CA: Dickenson, 1976),
83-97. Ian Barbour, furthermore, has been especially
helpful in showing that it is difficult to draw the line
between scientific "truths" and religious "myths," for in
fact both scientific and religious beliefs are based on
non-literal conceptualizations of reality as it is
experienced physically and intuitively. See Barbour's
Myths, Models and Paradigms (New York: Harper and Row,
1974), and his Issues in Science and Religion (New York:
Harper and Row, 1971); see also the classic by Thomas S.
Kuhn, The Structure of Scientific Revolutions (Chicago:
University of Chicago Press, 1962).

22. Hick, Evil and the God of Love, 249-250.

23. Hick, Evil and the God of Love, 250.

24. Satan has had an interesting history within biblical thought and the subsequent western Judaic-Christian tradition. He is the "angel of Yahweh" (Nm 22:22) who sets himself up as an "opposer" to Balaam. He patrols the earth and reports man's offenses to God (cf. Job 1:6-12; Ps 109:6; Zech 3:1-2; 1 Chr 21:1); in post-exilic times, however, he has become a bad angel who "tempts" human beings and seeks to bring about their downfall; he is identified also as the serpent in paradise (cf. Wis 2:24). In the New Testament, likewise, Satan (also called Beelsebub, Belial, the evil one, the accuser, the adversary, the enemy, etc.) is conceived as a fallen angel (cf. Lk 10:18) and as the great enemy of God who, as Lord of this world, tempts men to evil and deceit (Mt 4:3; 1 Thes 3:5; Cor 7:5; Jn 8:44) and causes various calamities. The evil spirits are under his control (Mt 25:41; 2 Cor 12:7; Eph 2:2); he is the serpent in paradise (2 Cor 11:3; Jn 8:44). His power, however, will be overcome, ultimately, by Christ. In post-biblical tradition, Satan's depiction as an evil power remains a dominant belief, sustained not only by official church doctrine but by literary classics like Milton's Paradise Lost, Goethe's Faust, and Byron's Cain. Recent movies depicting exorcisms indicate that belief in Satan as a personal power has survived into this century, despite theological efforts since the Enlightenment to demythologize him. See Schilling, God and Human Anguish, 108-113, and E. S. Gerstenberger and W. Schrage, Suffering (Nashville: Abingdon, 1977), 113-115 and 239-242. See also Encyclopedic Dictionary of the Bible (New York: McGraw-Hill, 1963), 2134-2137.

25. See Hick, Evil and the God of Love, 62-69; 119-126.

26. One can, of course, insist that there simply is no answer comprehensible to human beings and that, accordingly, we must accept this mystery in faith and awe. Yet this seems to be an abdication of our responsibilities to "think through" our beliefs, to seek as much understanding as we can. It may well be that we shall come to see that certain beliefs are inconsistent and dispensable if we are to construct a more viable religious world view.

27. See, for example, Gerstenberger and Schrage, Suffering, 240-242.

28. Gerstenberger and Schrage, Suffering, 241.

29. See Griffin, God, Power, and Evil, 31-37; and Gerstenberger and Schrage, Suffering, 235-239.

30. See also Schilling, God and Human Anguish, 55-72; Gerstenberger and Schrage, Suffering, 115-116.

31. See Robert N. Bellah, "Religious Evolution," American Sociological Review (1964), 358-374.

32. This may be an oversimplification, but I do not think it is misleading. See Alfred North Whitehead, Process and Reality (New York: Macmillan, 1929), 520.

33. Schubert Ogden, "Toward a New Theism," in D. Brown, R. E. James, and G. Reeves, eds., Process Philosophy and Christian Thought (Indianapolis and New York: Bobbs-Merrill, 1971), 176.

34. John A. T. Robinson, Honest to God (London: SCM, 1963), 123; see Schubert Ogden, The Reality of God (New York: Harper and Row, 1964), 19.

35. Alfred North Whitehead, Science and the Modern World (Toronto: Collier-Macmillan, 1967 [first edition, New York: Macmillan, 1925]), 189.

CHAPTER 3: RATIONAL SOLUTIONS

36. There are numerous descriptions of moral and physical evils. A particularly good one is given by McCloskey in Pike's book, God and Evil, 63-67. There are, of course, other ways to describe the world's evils (see, for example, Schilling, God and Human Anguish, 24-28), yet the two-fold division into moral and physical (or natural) evils seems to be the most widely used and accepted. See also Griffin, God, Power, and Evil, 27-28.

37. See Stephen Greenfield, "A Whiteheadian Perspective of the Problem of Evil: Whitehead's Understanding of Evil and Christian Theodicy," unpublished Ph.D. dissertation, Fordham University, 1973. Greenfield points to the distinction between a religious understanding of evil ("theodicy") and both a naturalistic understanding ("cosmodicy") and a humanistic understanding ("anthropodicy"), 10-57.

38. This point was made earlier. Our world view affects how we conceptualize God, and as our world view changes, so must our understanding of God, if it is to remain relevant and meaningful. The point is that our religious beliefs must be expressed in terms of some scientific-philosophical conceptuality. It has always been

so, and to appeal to the biblical writings without some
broader conceptuality seems rather stifling and unhelpful.
The Patristic era used Hellenistic conceptuality; Clement
and Origen accepted Middle Platonism, and Augustine
utilized Neo-Platonism. Aquinas later utilized the
Aristotelian framework. More contemporary thinkers use
Kant, Hegel, existentialism, or phenomenology, and so on.
Process thinkers, however, believe Whiteheadian process
metaphysics offers the most fruitful and valid
conceptuality. See Pittenger, Cosmic Love and Human Wrong,
11-12.

39. Alvin Plantinga, God, Freedom, and Evil (New
York: Harper and Row, 1974), 30.

40. Antony Flew, for example, contends that causal
determinism and freedom are not incompatible, a view shared
by Mackie. See Flew, "Divine Omnipotence and Human
Freedom," in A. Flew and Alasdair MacIntyre, eds., New
Essays in Philosophical Theology (London: SCM, 1955),
144-169; and J.L. Mackie, "Evil and Omnipotence," Mind
(1955), 200-212. This issue is discussed in Chapters 7 and
8. See also Plantinga, God, Freedom, and Evil, 31-34, and
passim; Clifford Williams, Free Will and Determinism: A
Dialogue (Indianapolis: Hackett, 1980); Bernard Berofsky,
ed., Free Will and Determinism (New York: Harper and Row,
1966); etc.

41. See Hick, Evil and the God of Love, 173.

42. See Schilling, God and Human Anguish, 119-145.

43. See Gerstenberger and Schrage, Suffering,
227-231.

44. See Chapter 6.

45. Heinrich Grüber, for example, believed that God
was active in the holocaust. Others, like Rubinstein, were
led to the opposite conclusion. See Galligan, God and
Evil, 8-9.

46. It is, of course, impossible to draw on
statistics to document this statement. Yet, as Schilling
and others have pointed out, it seems to be, beyond doubt,
the prevalent view that all things occur because of God's
providential will and plan. See Schilling, God and Human
Anguish, 55-67.

47. Jesus adds: "but unless you repent, you will
all come to the same end," and while this seems to
contradict what he has just said, it need not be
interpreted as such. Jesus rejects the view that the evil
which befalls us is due to divine punishment, but rather
than engaging in theological speculations as to an
alternative explanation, he merely uses the occasion to

issue a call to repentance. See Gerstenberger and Schrage, Suffering, 227-229.

48. See Chapter 8, where the issue of divine intervention is critically discussed.

49. I am not suggesting that empirical evidence can decide religious issues, yet surely it is not irrelevant.

50. Closely related to the explanation for evil as divine punishment is the biblical view that evil and suffering can be a means of expiation or atonement which softens the wrath of God.   One need only look to the laments in the Psalms, in the Book of Lamentations, and in Jeremiah and Habakkuk, etc., for an abundance of references to this belief.   In the Psalms especially, the illness, anguish, destruction, slander and ridicule, etc., which cause so much suffering "is not hidden, but is presented, in what to our taste often is a strong, obtrusive way, to the one who has caused it, or who is responsible for the wellbeing of those who worship him" (Gerstenberger and Schrage, Suffering, 107.   See also Daniel J. Simundson, Faith Under Fire [Minneapolis: Augsburg, 1980], 55-61). This explanation for evil seems to imply that the evil and suffering creatures endure can be removed by God if and when he sees fit--in response to the lamentations of his people. Yet the suffering presumably has been given by God in the first place, and it is just this conception of God to which process thinkers object: it seems inconsistent with divine benevolence and is an improper understanding of divine power, rendering problematic creaturely autonomy vis-à-vis the divine causal agency.

51. Joyce, Principles of Natural Theology, 596, cited by McCloskey, in Pike, God and Evil, 69.

52. See Gerstenberger and Schrage, Suffering, 215-218.

53. Schrage points out that suffering is not seen as a transforming power, that the assayer's fire does not forge a more pure and refined faith; rather, suffering brings out what a person already is, a patient or an impatient person.   See Gerstenberger and Schrage, Suffering, 217.

54. McCloskey, in Pike, God and Evil, 69.

55. A closely related view explains evil as divine educational discipline: "it is only through his own pain that man learns to stay within his limits and thereby to provide a basis for his happiness" (Gerstenberger and Schrage, Suffering, 110.   See also Simundson, Faith Under Fire, 130-132).   God sends his evils and afflictions,

supposedly, not because of human misconduct, but to help his creatures see their errors and return to the righteous path, and to its rewards. As Paul informs us, God "is disciplining us, to save us from being condemned with the rest of the world" (1 Cor 11:32). Likewise, we read in Deuteronomy that "the Lord your God is disciplining you as a father disciplines his son" and is thereby "bringing you to a rich land" (Deut 7:4-7). Again, in Proverbs: "My son, do not spurn the Lord's correction or take offense at his reproof; for those whom he loves the Lord reproves" (Prov 3:11-12). The author of the Book of Hebrews elaborates upon this theme:

> You have forgotten the text of Scripture which addresses you as sons and appeals to you in these words: "My son, do not think lightly of the Lord's discipline, nor lose heart when he corrects you; for the Lord disciplines those whom he loves; he lays the rod on every son whom he acknowledges:" You must endure it as discipline: God is treating you as sons. Can anyone be a son, who is not disciplined by his father? If you escape the discipline in which all sons share, you must be bastards and no true sons. Again, we paid due respect to the earthly fathers who disciplined us; should we not submit even more readily to our spiritual Father, and so attain life? They disciplined us for this short life according to their lights; but he does so for our true welfare, so that we may share his holiness. Discipline, no doubt, is never pleasant; at the time it seems painful, but in the end it yields for those who have been trained by it the peaceful harvest of an honest life (Heb 12:5-12).

Process thinkers would have no quarrel with the view that suffering can lead to good ends, or that one learns and is disciplined through suffering, and through it may return to the path desired by God. But to believe that God deliberately causes suffering for this reason is to hold an invalid conception of divine benevolence and of the divine causal agency in the world.

56. Simundson, _Faith Under Fire_, 68.

57. See Simundson, _Faith Under Fire_, 78.

58. See Gerstenberger and Schrage, _Suffering_, 180.

59. Gerstenberger and Schrage, _Suffering_, 181-182.

60. The point here is that it is difficult to understand why we must suffer for others. In Jesus' case the issue is clear, but in our case, do we suffer for others to build our own character, or is it a means whereby

we experience Christ, etc.? Paul sees his own suffering for the sake of spreading the Gospel (cf. Phil 1:12-14), and Isaiah 40-55 sees the suffering Jews as "a light to the nations." Yet, as Simundson points out, is it the case that "most human suffering has a potential value for others?" It would be difficult to bear this out in our actual experience. It would also seem hard to believe that most of our suffering (unlike that of first century Christians) has to do with an explicit committment to the faith. See Simundson, Faith Under Fire, 131-132.

61. See Schilling, God and Human Anguish, 174-192.

62. See Arthur O. Lovejoy, The Great Chain of Being (Cambridge: Harvard University Press, 1936).

63. Cited by Hick, Evil and the God of Love, 74.

64. Cited by Griffin, God, Power, and Evil, 85.

65. New species are slowly being created in the evolutionary advance. The modern world view is dynamic and, therefore, difficult to reconcile with the principle of plenitude. A number of other criticisms of this principle are raised by Hick in his Evil and the God of Love, 76-82; Schilling likewise raises several seemingly legitimate criticisms and concludes that "the principle of plenitude contributes little of value to our understanding either of evil or reality as a whole." See his God and Human Anguish, 232-234. It is, for example, difficult to believe that the inequalities which exist on the human level--the differences between genius and retardation, between good and poor opportunities, between health and sickness, and so on--are demanded by the need for fullness of being. "Much injustice seems to be involved," to say the least.

66. See Farrer's Love Almighty and Ills Unlimited (New York: Doubleday, 1961 and London: Collins, 1962), 49-76.

67. Whitehead writes: "The ultimate evil in the temporal world . . . lies in the fact that the past fades, that time is a 'perpetual perishing'" (Process and Reality, 517). Every new actualization of value excludes other potential values and this exclusion is loss. Often higher values are lost as lesser values are actualized.

68. See Chapter 9 for a discussion of the aesthetic considerations utilized in process theodicy.

69. See Schilling, God and Human Anguish, 146-173.

70. Hick, Evil and the God of Love, 253-261, and his "An Irenaean Theodicy," in Davis, ed., Encountering Evil, 41-42. A more sophisticated version is given by Pierre

Teilhard de Chardin. He proposes a scheme wherein creation procedes through five stages: "cosmogenesis" (the creation of physical matter); "biogenesis" (the evolution of organic life); "noogenesis" (the evolution of conscious beings); "planetization" (the population of the planet by human beings); and finally, the stage in which we now exist, "Christogenesis," and in which we have the opportunity to perfect our spiritual capabilities. For an excellent summary of Teilhard's teaching, see Roger A. Johnson, Ernest Wallwork, and others, Critical Issues in Modern Religion (Englewood Cliffs: Prentice-Hall, 1973), 114-140.

71. Hick's understanding of divine omnipotence is consistent with traditional theism: God is the actual or potential controller of all events and he could directly intervene (if he wished) to prevent any particular instance of suffering. Hick believes that God will not intervene because to do so would be to negate (at least temporarily) creaturely autonomy and thus defeat God's soul-making purpose for us. The process thinkers' position differs markedly from this in that they regard as invalid any possibility of creatures existing without freedom (or at least, for the more primitive levels of creatures, without genuine spontaneity), an autonomy that even God cannot override. See Griffin, God, Power, and Evil, 174-204.

72. Hick has responded to criticisms of this sort, yet not always successfully. To Hare and Madden's protest that the price of soul-making is too high in destructive evil, Hick, for example, appeals to the belief (rejected by Dostoevski in The Brothers Karamazov) that there can be "a future good so great as to render acceptable, in retrospect, the whole human experience, with all its wickedness and suffering" (Hick, Evil and the God of Love, 386; see 365-386). Elsewhere, Hick comes closer to a more promising response. Suppose, he suggests, that there were no disproportionate suffering, that wrong deeds would bring disaster upon the agent and good deeds would bring immediate rewards. But "in such a world truly moral action done because it is right, would be impossible;" we would act with rewards and punishments in mind, rather than doing good for its own sake. Such a world could not be a place for the development of our spiritual natures. See Hick's "An Irenaean Theodicy," 50.

73. See Hick, Evil and the God of Love, 82-89.

74. Hare and Madden, Evil and the Concept of God, 62.

75. Hare and Madden, Evil and the Concept of God, 63-64.

76. See F. Dostoevski, The Brothers Karamazov, part of which is cited in Pike, God and Evil, 6-16. Despite the New Testament's belief in a post mortem life, there are serious questions to be raised about it. Appeals to personal immortality do not justify or compensate the world's evils. See Schilling, God and Human Anguish, 172-173; 273-274. Schilling's point, shared by process thinkers, is surely valid: "belief in everlasting life is not in itself a sufficient answer to evil, since no future blessedness can justify the intensity and duration of the terrors that many people must endure here and now." His qualifying sentence, however, would be challenged by process thinkers: "But without that belief, the other considerations, however weighty, remain also inadequate" (273). See Chapter 9.

77. See Chapter 9.

78. Charles Hartshorne, The Divine Relativity: A Social Conception of God (New Haven: Yale University Press, 1948), 136.

CHAPTER 4: PROCESS THEODICY

79. Hartshorne has pointed out a number of historical thinkers who, in one way or another, have not espoused the traditional theism and who can be seen (somewhat) as forerunners of process thought. Among them are Fausto Socinus, F. W. J. von Schelling, W.P. Montague, Jules Lequier, G. T. Fechner, Henri Bergson, John Dewey, William James, etc. See Charles Hartshorne, "Ideas and Theses of Process Philosophers," in L. S. Ford, ed., Two Process Philosophers: Hartshorne's Encounter with Whitehead (Tallahassee: American Academy of Religion, 1973), 100-103; Charles Hartshorne and William Reese, eds., Philosophers Speak of God (Chicago: University of Chicago Press, 1953), 233-234; Charles Hartshorne, A Natural Theology for our Time (La Salle: Open Court, 1967), vii-viii; etc.

80. Griffin, God, Power, and Evil, 16-17.

81. Hartshorne, "A New Look at the Problem of Evil," 202. Hartshorne argues that "[t]he entire ancient world produced no clear alternative to the monopoly notion of unsurpassable power" (Natural Theology, 120).

82. See Griffin, God, Power, and Evil, passim.

83. See Chapter 6.

84. See Chapter 6.

85. Whitehead, Process and Reality, 341. I have equated "natural laws" with the "metaphysical categories," and while this may not be strictly accurate, the differences are not so essential as to invalidate the point I wish to make.

CHAPTER 5: EVIL AND GOD'S NECESSARY EXISTENCE

86. See Charles Hartshorne, "Can There Be Proofs for the Existence of God?," in Robert H. Ayers and William T. Blackstone, eds., Religious Language and Knowledge (Athens: University of Georgia Press, 1972), 62.

87. See Hartshorne, "Can There Be Proofs?," 66-67.

88. Hartshorne, Natural Theology, 31.

89. Hartshorne, Natural Theology, 32.

90. Hartshorne, "Can There Be Proofs?," 65.

91. Hartshorne, Natural Theology, 33.

92. Charles Hartshorne, Creative Synthesis and Philosophic Method (La Salle: Open Court, 1970), 229.

93. Hartshorne, Creative Synthesis, 277.

94. See Chapter 6.

95. Hartshorne, Natural Theology, 71-72.

96. Hartshorne, Natural Theology, 29.

97. Hartshorne, Natural Theology, 30.

98. Hartshorne, "Can There Be Proofs?," 68.

99. Hartshorne, Creative Synthesis, 290.

100. Hartshorne, Creative Synthesis, 281.

101. Hartshorne, Creative Synthesis, 280.

102. Hartshorne, "Can There Be Proofs?," 75.

103. Hartshorne, "Can There Be Proofs?," 68.

104. See, for example, Hick's explanation:
     The theistic arguments are commonly distinguished as being either a priori or a posteriori. An a posteriori argument is

one which relies on a premise derived from
(hence after, or posterior to) experience.
Accordingly a posteriori arguments for the
existence of God infer a deity from
evidences within our human experience. An a
priori argument on the other hand operates
from a basis which is logically prior to and
independent of experience. It rests on
solely logical considerations and (if it
succeeds) achieves the kind of certainty
exhibited by mathematical truths.

Hick adds that "only one strictly a priori proof has been
offered--the ontological argument of Anselm, Descartes, and
others" (John Hick, ed., The Existence of God [London:
Collier-Macmillan, 1964], 3).

105. See Hartshorne, Natural Theology, 17-18; see
also Charles Hartshorne, "What Did Anselm Discover?," in
John Hick and Arthur McGill, eds., The Many-Faced Argument
(London: Macmillan, 1968), 321-333; and Charles
Hartshorne, Anselm's Discovery (La Salle: Open Court,
1965), passim.

106. Hartshorne, Natural Theology, 67-68.

107. Charles Hartshorne, "God's Existence: A Conceptual Problem," in Sidney Hook, ed., Religious Experience
and Truth (New York: New York University Press,
1961), 217-218.

108. See Eugene Peters, Hartshorne and Neoclassical
Metaphysics (Lincoln: University of Nebraska Press, 1970),
75.

109. Hartshorne, Anselm's Discovery, 135.

110. Hartshorne, Creative Synthesis, 276.

111. Hartshorne, Natural Theology, 88.

112. Hartshorne, Natural Theology, 52.

113. Hartshorne, "Can There Be Proofs?," 68.

114. Hartshorne, Natural Theology, 30.

115. Hartshorne, Natural Theology, 31.

116. Hartshorne, Natural Theology, 30.

117. Hartshorne, "Can There Be Proofs?," 68.

118. Hartshorne, "Can There Be Proofs?," 68-69. See
also Hartshorne, Creative Synthesis, 284.

119. Hartshorne, "Can There Be Proofs?," 69.

120. See Hartshorne, Philosophers Speak of God, 273-274.

121. Hartshorne, "Can There Be Proofs?," 69.

122. Hartshorne, Natural Theology, 59.

123. Hartshorne, "Can There Be Proofs?," 69.

124. See Hartshorne, Natural Theology, 54.

125. Hartshorne, Natural Theology, 56.

126. See Hartshorne, "Can There Be Proofs?," 71.

127. Hartshorne, "Can There Be Proofs?," 71.

128. Hartshorne, "Can There Be Proofs?," 71.

129. Hartshorne, Creative Synthesis, 289.

130. Hartshorne, Creative Synthesis, 289.

131. Hartshorne, "Can There Be Proofs?," 71.

132. Hartshorne has written two books and several articles on the ontological proof and has probably done more than anyone to reopen discussion on this proof. See his Anselm's Discovery and The Logic of Perfection and Other Essays in Neoclassical Metaphysics (La Salle: Open Court, 1962). See also George L. Goodwin, The Ontological Argument of Charles Hartshorne (Missoula, MT; Scholars Press, 1978).

133. Hartshorne, "What Did Anselm Discover?," 322.

134. Hartshorne, "What Did Anselm Discover?," 322.

135. Hartshorne, "What Did Anselm Discover?," 322.

136. See, for example, Hartshorne, Man's Vision of God, 6.

137. See Hartshorne, "What Did Anselm Discover?," 326.

138. Hartshorne, "Can There Be Proofs?," 74.

139. Hartshorne, "What Did Anselm Discover?," 327.

140. Hartshorne, "What Did Anselm Discover?," 326.

141. See Hartshorne, "What Did Anselm Discover?," 327-328. See also Hartshorne, Logic of Perfection, 46; etc. Hartshorne's critique of "positivism" is found throughout many of his writings: see especially Anselm's Discovery, passim, and Beyond Humanism (Lincoln: University of Nebraska Press, 1937), 253-297.

142. Charles Hartshorne, "The Formal Validity and Real Significance of the Ontological Argument," The

Philosophical Review (1944), 229. See also Hartshorne, Philosophers Speak of God, 97; and his "What the Ontological Proof Does Not Do," Review of Metaphysics (1964), 608-609.

143. Hartshorne, "Formal Validity," 228.

144. Hartshorne, "What Did Anselm Discover?," 328.

145. See Hartshorne, Natural Theology, 19-20; 42-43.

146. See Hartshorne, Natural Theology, 71.

147. It is at this point that one of the major areas of divergence between Hartshorne and Whitehead appears. While Whitehead envisages "eternal objects" as specific ideals, eternally distinct and definite possibilities, Hartshorne postulates that there is, rather, only a general continuum of possibility which is indeterminate until rendered determinate by selective creaturely actualizations. See Charles Hartshorne, Whitehead's Philosophy: Selected Essays, 1935-1970 (Lincoln: University of Nebraska Press, 1973), 31; Hartshorne, Creative Synthesis, 57-68; and "Interrogation of Charles Hartshorne," in Sydney and Beatrice Rome, eds., Philosophical Interrogations (New York and Evanston: Harper and Row, 1964), 347. See also David Griffin, "Hartshorne's Differences from Whitehead," and Lewis Ford, "Whitehead's Differences from Hartshorne," in Ford, Two Process Philosophers, 37-40; 58-65. Also see Barry L. Whitney, "Does God Influence the World's Creativity?: Hartshorne's Doctrine of Possibility," Philosophy Research Archives (1981), 613-622; Eugene Peters, "Hartshorne on Actuality, "Process Studies (1977), 200-204; and Richard E. Creel, "Continuity, Possibility, and Omniscience," Process Studies (1982), 209-231.

148. Hartshorne, Philosophers Speak of God, 10.

149. Hartshorne, "Can There Be Proofs?," 74.

150. Hartshorne's argument is that "metaphysical truths" are such "that no experience can contradict them" and "that any experience can illustrate them" (Logic of Perfection, 285). "Something exists" is the most basic of such truths. It is necessarily true since it is unfalsifiable and yet verifiable at every moment. Other metaphysical truths are that "some experience occurs," that "creative synthesis occurs," and that "divine or infallible experience, having fallible experiences among its objects, occurs." Infallible experience is not falsifiable by fallible experience, nor can it falsify itself, and Hartshorne believes it is verified also by our fallible experiences. This last claim, to be sure, appeals to

mystical experiences and to the theistic proofs. See Hartshorne's detailed elaboration and defence of this contention in Creative Synthesis, 159-172. See also the commentaries by William O'Meara, "Hartshorne's Interpretation of Whitehead's Methodology," in Ford, Two Process Philosophers, 84-88; and George Goodwin, The Ontological Argument of Charles Hartshorne, 13-30.

151. Hartshorne, "Can There Be Proofs?," 75. See also Hartshorne, Natural Theology, 67.

152. See Hartshorne, "What Did Anselm Discover?," 328.

153. See Hartshorne, "What Did Anselm Discover?," 329.

154. See Peters, Hartshorne and Neoclassical Metaphysics, 69; and Colin Gunton, Becoming and Being: The Doctrine of God in Charles Hartshorne and Karl Barth (Oxford: Oxford University Press, 1978), 100.

155. See Hartshorne, Logic of Perfection, 103; and Peters, Hartshorne, 68.

156. Hartshorne, "A New Look at the Problem of Evil," 201.

157. Hartshorne, "A New Look at the Problem of Evil," 202.

158. Griffin, God, Power, and Evil, 256.

159. Hartshorne, "Ideas and Theses," 102.

160. John Cobb, "'Perfection Exists': A Critique of Charles Hartshorne," Religion in Life (1963), 302.

PART TWO: THE PROCESS GOD

CHAPTER 6: GOD AS PROCESSIVE

1. Charles Hartshorne and Creighton Peden, Whitehead's View of Reality (New York: The Pilgrim Press, 1981), 12. Hartshorne suggests elsewhere that the traditional theism can be "summed up in the Thomistic phrase, 'pure actuality' (actus purus)--or, in the more modern expression, 'the absolute' --implying a being solely actual, or wholly unrelated:" see his The Divine Relativity: A Social Conception of God (New Haven: Yale University Press, 1948), 3. See also David Griffin's discussion of traditional theism in his God, Power, and Evil: A Process Theodicy (Philadelphia: Westminster, 1976), 73-77; and James Keller, "Some Basic Differences Between Classical and Process Metaphysics and their Implications for the Concept of God," International Philosophical Quarterly (1982), 9-10.

2. Charles Hartshorne and William Reese, eds., Philosophers Speak of God (Chicago: The University of Chicago Press, 1953), 20.

3. Hartshorne, Divine Relativity, 58.

4. See Alfred North Whitehead, Process and Reality (New York: Macmillan, 1929), 28. See also 27-94. The corrected edition by David Griffin and D. W. Sherburne (New York: The Free Press, 1978) is more useful.

5. See F. B. Wallack, The Epochal Nature of Process in Whitehead's Metaphysics (Albany: The State University of New York Press, 1980), 7-46.

6. See, for example, Charles Hartshorne, "Personal Identity from A to Z," Process Studies (1972), 209-215; and

his "Strict and Genetic Identity: An Illustration of the Relations of Logic to Metaphysics," in Horace M. Kallen, et al, Structure, Method, and Meaning: Essays in Honor of Henry M. Sheffer (New York: Liberal Arts Press, 1951), 242-254. There has been an active debate concerning the viability of the conception of personal identity in process thought. See, for example, Albert Shalom and John C. Robertson, Jr., "Hartshorne and the Problem of Personal Identity," Process Studies (1978), 169-179; D. Browning, "Whitehead's Theory of Human Agency," Dialogue (1963-64), 424-441; John Bennett, "Whitehead and Personal Identity," The Thomist (1973), 510-521; Frank Kirkpatrick, "Process or Agent: Models of Self and God," Thought (1973), 33-60; etc.

7. See, for example, Charles Hartshorne, Creative Synthesis and Philosophic Method (London: SCM Press, 1970), 45-46; 173-204; and his The Logic of Perfection and Other Essays in Neoclassical Metaphysics (La Salle: Open Court, 1962), 218-219; see also James A. Keller, "Some Basic Differences Between Classical and Process Metaphysics," 6-8, which contrasts the substance doctrine of traditional metaphysics with the process doctrine.

8. Hartshorne, Philosophers Speak of God, 2.

9. Charles Hartshorne, "Panpsychism," in V. Ferm, ed., A History of Philosophical Systems (New York: Philosophical Library, 1950), 451.

10. Schubert Ogden, The Reality of God (New York: Harper and Row, 1964), 57.

11. See Charles Hartshorne, Whitehead's Philosophy: Selected Essays, 1935-1970 (Lincoln: University of Nebraska Press, 1973), 68-70.

12. For a useful discussion of Hartshorne's dipolar theism, see Colin E. Gunton, Becoming and Being (Oxford: Oxford University Press, 1978), 24-35; see also Edward Farley, The Transcendence of God (Philadelphia: Westminster, 1958), 130-161; and two books by Eugene Peters: The Creative Advance (St. Louis: The Bethany Press, 1966), 77-104; and Hartshorne and Neoclassical Metaphysics (Lincoln: The University of Nebraska Press, 1970), 59-76.

13. Hartshorne, Philosophers Speak of God, 3.

14. Hartshorne, Philosophers Speak of God, 3.

15. Charles Hartshorne, Man's Vision of God and the Logic of Theism (Chicago: Willett, Clark and Company, 1941; reprinted by Archon Books, Hamden, Conn., 1964), 165.

16. Hartshorne, Man's Vision of God, 164.

17. John C. Robertson, Jr., "Does God Change?," _Ecumenist_ (1971), 63.

18. W. Norris Clarke, "A New Look at the Immutability of God," in R. J. Roth, ed., _God Knowable and Unknowable_ (New York: Fordham University Press, 1973), 44.

19. Clarke, "A New Look at the Immutability of God," 48. Hartshorne rejects this logic: "Can a thing," he asks, "be in relation and yet be exactly as it would be if it were not in relation?" Is it not more meaningful to argue that "what knowledge the divine has must be one thing if it creates (or if there exists) this world, and another thing if it creates that world?" (_Divine Relativity_, 6, 11).

20. James W. Felt, "Invitation to a Philosophic Revolution," _New Scholasticism_ (1971), 98-99.

21. John C. Robertson, Jr., _The Concept of the Divine Person in the Thought of Charles Hartshorne and Karl Barth_, unpublished Ph.D. Dissertation (Yale University, 1968), 33.

22. Hartshorne, _Whitehead's View of Reality_, 13. See also Gunton, _Becoming and Being_, 17-18; and Ogden, _The Reality of God_, 17-18.

23. "If God knows what is future to man as a Now, in what sense is it really future, and what would prevent the whole experience of process from being mere illusion? If time is real, future cannot be reduced to the state of the present, for the very meaning of present depends on the open possibility of actualizing future states." See Farley, _The Transcendence of God_, 133-134; and Charles Hartshorne, "Contingency and the New Era in Metaphysics," _Journal of Philosophy_ (1932), 458.

24. For an overview of the recent discussions, see Barry L. Whitney, "Divine Immutability in Process Philosophy and Contemporary Thomism," _Horizons_ (1980), 49-68. This article has occasioned, in part, an interesting dialogue between David Burrell and Philip Devenish, in _Theological Studies_ (1982), 125-135 and 504-513.

25. Clarke, "A New Look at the Immutability of God," 45. See also his more recent, _The Philosophical Approach to God: A Contemporary Neo-Thomist Perspective_ (Winston-Salem: Wake Forest University Publications, 1979), 66-109.

26. Felt, "Invitation," 99, 108.

27. Felt, "Invitation," 96.

28. Felt, "Invitation," 104.

29. Joseph Donceel, "Second Thoughts on the Nature of God," Thought (1971), 347.

30. Donceel, "Second Thoughts," 349.

31. Donceel, "Second Thoughts," 355.

32. Piet Schoonenberg, "Process or History in God?," Louvain Studies (1973), 316.

33. Piet Schoonenberg, Man and Sin (Notre Dame: University of Notre Dame Press, 1965), 50.

34. Walter Stokes, "Freedom as Perfection: Whitehead, Thomas and Augustine," Proceedings of the American Catholic Philosophical Association (1962), 134. See also the following by Stokes: "Is God Really Related to this World?," Proceedings of the American Catholic Philosophical Association (1965), 145-151; "God for Today and Tomorrow," New Scholasticism (1963), 351-378; and "Whitehead's Challenge to Theistic Realism," New Scholasticism (1964), 1-21.

35. William Hill, "Does the World Make a Difference to God?," The Thomist (1974), 146, emphasis added. See also his "Two Gods of Love: Aquinas and Whitehead," Listening (1976), 249-264; and his "Does God Know the Future?: Aquinas and Some Moderns," Theological Studies (1975), 3-18.

36. Hill, "Does the World Make a Difference to God?," 147.

37. John Wright, "Divine Knowledge and Human Freedom: The God Who Dialogues," Theological Studies (1977), 450.

38. Wright, "Divine Knowledge," 458.

39. Anthony Kelly, "God: How Near a Relation?," The Thomist (1970), 193.

40. Kelly, "God: How Near a Relation?," 194-195.

41. Karl Rahner, Theological Investigations, IV (Baltimore: Helicon, 1966), 113-114. See also J. Norman King and Barry L. Whitney, "Rahner and Hartshorne on Divine Immutability," International Philosophical Quarterly (1982), 195-209, for a detailed discussion which compares and contrasts the interpretations of divine immutability in Rahner and Hartshorne.

42. Donceel, "Second Thoughts," 350.

43. See, for example, Clarke, "A New Look at the Immutability of God," 45; Hill, "Does the World Make a Difference to God?," 151; and Kelly, "God: How Near a Relation?," 203.

44. Clarke, "A New Look at the Immutability of God," 68.

45. Lewis S. Ford, "The Immutable God of Father Clarke," New Scholasticism (1975), 193.

46. Ford, "The Immutable God," 194. Clarke has responded in his Philosophical Approach to God, Chapter 3. In this later work, Clarke, on the one hand, makes important concessions to the process position on a few precise points, especially regarding God's real relation to the world (which he now accepts) and, on the other hand, suggests constructive ways in which process philosophy could be rendered more congenial to Thomistic metaphysics.

47. See Hartshorne, Divine Relativity, 48-49.

48. Hartshorne, Divine Relativity, 55.

49. Hartshorne, Divine Relativity, 55.

50. Charles Hartshorne, Reality as Social Process: Studies in Metaphysics and Religion (Glencoe: The Free Press and Boston: The Beacon Press, 1953, reprinted by Hafner, 1971), 40.

51. Hartshorne, Man's Vision of God, 117. Elsewhere Hartshorne writes: "To say, on the one hand, that God is love . . . and on the other to speak of an absolute, infinite, immutable, simple, impassive deity, is . . . a gigantic hoax;" "Either God really does love all beings, that is, is related to them by a sympathetic union . . . or religion is a vast fraud" (Divine Relativity, 26, 25).

52. See Hartshorne, Creative Synthesis, 237; and 226-244; see also his Philosophers Speak of God, 1-15; Alan Gragg, Charles Hartshorne (Waco: Word Books, 1973), 82-91; Farley, Transcendence, 146-157; and Lewis Ford, "Whitehead's Categoreal Derivation of Divine Existence," Monist (1969), 374-400.

53. Hartshorne, Divine Relativity, x.

54. Hartshorne, Divine Relativity, 74.

55. Hartshorne, Man's Vision of God, 234.

56. Hartshorne, Man's Vision of God, 233.

57. Hartshorne, Man's Vision of God, 230.

58. Hartshorne, Divine Relativity, 130.

59. Charles Hartshorne, "Could There Have Been a Nothing? A Reply," Process Studies (1971), 25.

60. Hartshorne, Man's Vision of God, 230.

61. Hartshorne, Man's Vision of God, 230-231.

62. Hartshorne, <u>Man's Vision of God</u>, 231.

63. Hartshorne, <u>Man's Vision of God</u>, 232.

64. Lewis Ford has addressed this issue from the perspective of Whitehead's thought, noting that while the world was not created <u>ex</u> <u>nihilo</u>, the question is whether the world which has always existed exists necessarily or contingently, dependent upon a divine creative act. Ford argues that for Whitehead it is the latter. For Hartshorne, however, it is not clear that this can be maintained. Unlike Whitehead, Hartshorne assumes that the metaphysical structure of the world necessarily exists as embodied at all times and that it lacks any consistent alternative (although the laws of nature God imposes on this world vary in different cosmic epochs). Whitehead assumed, on the other hand, that alternative metaphysical structures <u>are</u> consistently conceivable, "including one whereby his [God's] own act of existence would completely exhaust all creativity, permitting him to exist in his solitary splendor." The metaphysical structure God has chosen is in fact one in which "the world is required for the completion of God's experience, for God has chosen to be that sort of God who is enriched by the novelty and sociability of free subjectivities other than himself" ("Can Freedom Be Created?", <u>Horizons</u> [1977], 184-185). See also Ford, "The Viability of Whitehead's God for Christian Theism," <u>Proceedings of the American Catholic Philosophical Association</u> (1970), 141-153. For Hartshorne's treatment of this question see, for example, his <u>Man's Vision of God</u>, 230-250; <u>Whitehead's Philosophy</u>, 193-195; <u>The Logic of Perfection</u>, 273-275; and his "Could There Have Been a Nothing?: A Reply," 25-28.

CHAPTER 7: GOD AS PERSUASIVE

65. Alfred North Whitehead, <u>Religion in the Making</u> (New York: Macmillan, 1926), 55, 74-75; <u>Science and the Modern World</u> (New York: Macmillan, 1925), 266.

66. Alfred North Whitehead, <u>Modes of Thought</u> (New York: Macmillan, 1938), 68.

67. Alfred North Whitehead, <u>Adventures of Ideas</u> (New York: Macmillan, 1933), 218; <u>Dialogues of Alfred North Whitehead</u>, as recorded by Lucien Price (Boston: Little, Brown, 1954), 176, 198, 277.

68. Whitehead, <u>Adventures of Ideas</u>, 213.

69. Whitehead, Adventures of Ideas, 213. See William Christian, An Interpretation of Whitehead's Metaphysics (New Haven: Yale University Press, 1959), 388-390, from which the references listed in notes 65-69 were taken.

70. Whitehead, Process and Reality, 519-520.

71. Whitehead, Process and Reality, 520.

72. See Gunton, Becoming and Being, 17-18.

73. Gunton, Becoming and Being, 17. Gunton accurately summarizes Hartshorne's position: "There can surely be no defence against the charge that a wholly necessary God and a free creation are logically incompatible. If God has to be free in order to create...then, however much the word necessary is qualified, it is impossible to reconcile this freedom with the demands of a thoroughgoing necessity" (18).

74. See Hartshorne, Divine Relativity, 116-117; and Griffin, God, Power, and Evil, 73-77.

75. Griffin, God, Power, and Evil, passim.

76. Griffin, God, Power, and Evil, 60.

77. Griffin, God, Power, and Evil, 60-61.

78. Griffin, God, Power, and Evil, 60. I am aware that this is a contentious point, and that some writers insist that God's knowing of the future does not negate our freedom. I have, however, never seen the logic of this position. See B. Brody, ed., Readings in the Philosophy of Religion (Englewood Cliffs: Prentice-Hall, 1974), 364-427. See especially the chapter by William Rowe, "Augustine on Foreknowledge and Free Will," 384-389.

79. See John Hick, Evil and the God of Love (New York: Harper and Row, 1966, revised edition, 1978), 266-277; see also Antony Flew, "Divine Omnipotence and Human Freedom," in A. Flew and A. MacIntyre, eds., New Essays in Philosophical Theology (London: SCM Press, 1955), 144-169; and J. L. Mackie, "Evil and Omnipotence," Mind (1955), 200-212. Griffin has rightly rejected this view as it is defended by Hick, for in concurring with Flew and Mackie that freedom is compatible with character-determinism, Hick undercuts the plausibility of his argument that God is justified in creating a world in which genuine evil is possible. According to the Flew-Mackie view, "we would be free, and go through a slow learning process, complete with real temptations, without the real possibility of sinning." See Griffin, God, Power, and Evil, 182.

80. Augustine, Enchiridion, XCVI, CII, XCV, in Whitney J. Oates, ed., Basic Writings of St. Augustine (New York: Random House, 1948), 713, 718, 713. See Griffin, God, Power, and Evil, 62-63.

81. Augustine, Enchiridion, C, 717. See Griffin, God, Power, and Evil, 63.

82. Augustine, Enchiridion, CIII, 718. See Griffin, God, Power, and Evil, 64.

83. Augustine, On Grace and Free Will, XLII, in Basic Writings of St. Augustine, 769. See Griffin, God, Power, and Evil, 64.

84. Augustine, On the Predestination of the Saints, XXII, in Basic Writings of St. Augustine, 797. See Griffin, God, Power, and Evil, 65.

85. Griffin, God, Power, and Evil, 66.

86. Augustine, On Free Will, III, 48, in John H. S. Burleigh, translator, Augustine: Earlier Writings (London: SCM Press, 1953), 200; and Augustine, Confessions, VII (New York: The Modern Library, 1949), 122. See Hick, Evil and the God of Love, 59.

87. See Hick, Evil and the God of Love, 61.

88. See Griffin, God, Power, and Evil, 58. The Augustinian teaching may be summarized as follows: before the fall, man could either sin or not sin (posse peccare or posse non peccare); after the fall, he can only sin (non posse non peccare); but after grace, he can no longer sin (non posse peccare). This obviously is an oversimplification of the great profundity of the Augustinian position, and yet, in my opinion, it is hardly misleading.

89. Hick makes this point in his Evil and the God of Love, which contrasts the dominant Augustinian theodicy with the much neglected Irenaean alternative. See also Michael Galligan, God and Evil (New York: Paulist Press, 1976).

90. See Griffin, God, Power, and Evil, 78-79.

91. Hartshorne, Divine Relativity, 135. See also Griffin, God, Power and Evil, 80-84.

92. Martin Luther, On the Bondage of the Will, 614-620, in Luther and Erasmus: Free Will and Salvation (Philadelphia: Westminster, 1969), 119. See Griffin, God, Power, and Evil, 103.

93. Luther, On the Bondage of the Will, 786-787, 332. See Griffin, God, Power, and Evil, 105.

94. Luther, On the Bondage of the Will, 614-620, 118. See Griffin, God, Power, and Evil, 103.

95. Luther, On the Bondage of the Will, 618-620, 122. See Griffin, God, Power, and Evil, 106. Luther's position, while denying free will, has its own inner logic: salvation is solely God's work, not the work of human beings. We must trust, accordingly, in God's rule and plan. Yet as to why God permits so much evil and misery, Luther recommends that we not "ask this question, but . . . adore these mysteries. And if flesh and blood is offended here and murmurs (cf. John 6:61), by all means let it murmur; but it will achieve nothing; God will not change on that account" (On the Bondage of the Will, 709-714, 236). See Griffin, God, Power, and Evil, 109. It is much the same for Calvin: God's election of some of us to grace and others to disgrace and damnation is "dreadful," and yet we must "tremble with Paul at so deep a mystery;" the divine will "is higher than man's standard can measure, or than man's slender wit can comprehend" (John Calvin, Institutes of the Christian Religion, III, xxii, 1; and III, xxiii, 4, J. T. McNeill, ed. [Philadephia: Westminster, 1960], 955, 987, 952). See Griffin, God, Power, and Evil, 123-124.

96. Calvin, Institutes, I, xvi, 3, 200; and III, xxiii, 7, 955. See Griffin, God, Power, and Evil, 116-117.

97. Calvin, Institutes, III, xxiii, 7, 955-956. See Hick, Evil and the God of Love, 120.

98. Calvin, Institutes, III, xxiii, 8, 957. See Griffin, God, Power, and Evil, 120.

99. Hick, Evil and the God of Love, 121. See note 79.

100. See Griffin, God, Power, and Evil, 119-130; and Hick, Evil and the God of Love, 266-277. Belief in divine predestination certainly has not ended with the Reformers. It has continued, largely unabated, into contemporary Christianity. In the Westminster Confession, for example, "which is still the official standard of the English-speaking churches in the Reformed or Calvinist tradition. . .the chapter on God's eternal decrees has a very prominent place, prior even to that on creation, and is far separated from the chapters on salvation" (See Hick, Evil and the God of Love, 125). The "Thirty-Nine Articles" of the Church of England likewise hold to the belief in a divine predestination of all human beings (Article 17) and the belief that human free will "cannot turn" by its "own

natural strength, but must rely solely upon God's grace"
(Article 10): See The Book of Common Prayer (Toronto: The
Anglican Book Center, 1959), 698-714.

101. Whitehead, Adventures of Ideas, 213.

102. Whitehead, Religion in the Making, 57.

103. Hartshorne, Divine Relativity, 142.

104. Hartshorne, Divine Relativity, 154.

105. Charles   Hartshorne,   "Religion   in   Process
Philosophy," in F. C. Feaver and William Horosz, eds.,
Religion   in   Philosophical   and   Cultural   Perspective
(Princeton: D. Van Nostrand, 1967), 258.

106. Hartshorne, Creative Synthesis, 8.

107. Hartshorne, "Religion in Process Philosophy,"
261.

108. Hartshorne, "Religion in Process Philosophy,"
262.

109. Hartshorne, "Religion in Process Philosophy,"
261.

110. Charles Hartshorne, "A New Look at the Problem
of Evil," in F. C. Dommeyer, ed., Current Philosophical
Issues: Essays   in   Honor   of   Curt   John   Ducasse
(Springfield: C. C. Thomas, 1966), 209.

111. Hartshorne, Divine Relativity, 138.

112. Hartshorne, "A New Look at the Problem of Evil,"
210.

113. Hartshorne, Divine Relativity, 134.

114. Hartshorne, Creative Synthesis, 239.

115. My focus here is on Hartshorne's writings. I
suggest, however, that much of this discussion may apply to
Whitehead as well (and to the process literature in
general). The issue as to how God and creatures interact,
that is, with what degree of divine persuasiveness and/or
coerciveness, demands far greater attention and precision.
For some references to those thinkers who have addressed
the persuasion--coercion issue in process thought, see
note 148.

116. Hartshorne, "A New Look at the Problem of Evil,"
206. Hartshorne refers to these limits, variously, as "the
world order," "the laws of nature," "divine decrees"
(Creative Synthesis, 125); the "basic order" ("Abstract and
Concrete in God: A Reply," Review of Metaphysics [1963],
291); as the "natural or cosmic laws" ("A New Look at the

Problem of Evil," 209); as the "cosmic stabilities" ("A
Philosopher's Assessment of Christianity," in Walter
Leibrecht, ed., Religion and Culture: Essays in Honor of
Paul Tillich [New York: Harper, 1959], 177); etc. "The
only 'acts of God' we can identify (in spite of the
lawyers) are the laws of nature." (Charles Hartshorne, A
Natural Theology for Our Time [La Salle: Open Court,
1967], 102).

117. Charles Hartshorne, "Process and the Nature of
God," in G. F. McLean, ed., Traces of God in a Secular
Culture (New York: Alba House, 1973), 173. (Hartshorne
here refers to Whitehead, with whom he concurs).

118. Hartshorne, Whitehead's Philosophy, 164.

119. Hartshorne, "A New Look at the Problem of Evil,"
209.

120. Hartshorne, Philosophers Speak of God, 273-274.
(Hartshorne's reference here is to Whitehead's teaching,
with which he concurs).

121. Hartshorne, Divine Relativity, 135.

122. Hartshorne, The Logic of Perfection, 203-204.

123. Hartshorne, "A New Look at the Problem of Evil,"
209.

124. See Hartshorne, Logic of Perfection, 296-297.
It is interesting to note here a major point of divergence
between Hartshorne and Whitehead, for while Hartshorne
believes that God imposes the natural laws, Whitehead sees
them as "immanent" (see Lewis Ford, "Whitehead's
Differences from Hartshorne," in Lewis Ford, ed., Two
Process Philosophers: Hartshorne's Encounter with
Whitehead [Tallahasse: AAR Studies in Religion, 1973],
75-79). Whitehead's theory seems to me to be more
consistent with a "persuasive" God since the notion of
immanent laws implies that "the order of nature expresses
the characters of the real things which jointly compose the
existences of the world" (Whitehead, Adventures of Ideas,
142), rather than the laws being imposed upon creatures by
God. Yet, ultimately, Hartshorne's position may be the
more valid since, as he argues, without God's (coercive)
imposition of natural laws as the limits to creaturely
freedom, it is difficult to comprehend how a world order
could in fact come to exist. Is it not the case,
furthermore, as Whitehead himself acknowledged, that "apart
from some notion of imposed law, the doctrine of immanence
provides absolutely no reason why the universe should not
be steadily relapsing into lawless chaos"? (Adventures of
Ideas, 146). Yet Whitehead believed that divine persuasion

can maintain the world order, and while Hartshorne insists
that his God likewise persuades the world to maintain its
order, my argument has been that Hartshorne's God seems (in
this respect at least) to act coercively.

125. Hartshorne, "A New Look at the Problem of Evil,"
210.

126. Hartshorne, Creative Synthesis, 51, 166.

127. Hartshorne writes: "there is no reason to
regard natural laws as eternal. Quite the contrary . . . .
As with artistic styles, the variations eventually become
trivial and a new style is in order, for which reason at
due intervals God has to inspire the universe with new
modes of behavior" ("Process and the Nature of God," 137);
see also his Creative Synthesis, 138, and Logic
of Perfection, 96.

128. See Lewis S. Ford, The Lure of God
(Philadelphia: Fortress Press, 1978), 17. Ford, however,
does agree that Hartshorne's God coercively imposes the
natural laws. See his "Whitehead's Differences from
Hartshorne", 75-81.

129. Hartshorne, "Religion in Process Philosophy,"
262.

130. Hartshorne, Philosophers Speak of God, 274.
(Here again Hartshorne approvingly notes Whitehead's
doctrine, as consistent with his own position).

131. Hartshorne, Creative Synthesis, 31-32.

132. Hartshorne, "Religion in Process Philosophy,"
258. See also Griffin's argument in "Creation Out of Chaos
and the Problem of Evil," in Stephen T. Davis, ed.,
Encountering Evil (Atlanta: John Knox Press, 1981),
112-114. Griffin points to the distinction, utilized in
process thought, among various types of entities:
low-grade enduring individuals (electrons, atoms, etc.),
high-grade enduring individuals (exclusively human beings),
and aggregates (rocks, trees, etc.). With respect to
low-grade individuals, God's influence is minimal, for they
have little power except largely to repeat their past
structures. God's persuasive influence over such beings is
a long, slow, evolutionary process. With human beings,
however, God's lure can be more dramatically effective,
for we have the freedom to effect major changes. We can
respond to God's lure, or we can reject it. With
aggregates--and it is this point which most concerns us at
the moment--God has no influence at all since aggregates
are merely groupings of actual entities without a dominant,

unifying member. "There is no way," accordingly, that "God can prevent that aggregate of molecules called a hurricane from devastating the towns in its path" (113). This hypothesis, of course, requires a rather complex justification, but such seems possible, utilizing process metaphysics.

133. Hartshorne, Creative Synthesis, 8.

134. Hartshorne, "Religion in Process Philosophy," 261.

135. Hartshorne, "Religion in Process Philosophy," 261.

136. Hartshorne, Divine Relativity, 140.

137. Hartshorne, "Religion in Process Philosophy," 257.

138. Hartshorne, Whitehead's Philosophy, 164.

139. Hartshorne, "Religion in Process Philosophy," 258.

140. Hartshorne, "Religion in Process Philosophy," 261.

141. Hartshorne, Divine Relativity, 139.

142. Hartshorne, Divine Relativity, 139.

143. Hartshorne, Divine Relativity, 142.

144. Hartshorne, "Religion in Process Philosophy," 258. (Here Hartshorne refers to Whitehead's teaching, in agreement with his own).

145. Hartshorne, "Religion in Process Philosophy," 261.

146. Hartshorne, "A New Look at the Problem of Evil," 211.

147. Hartshorne, Divine Relativity, 142.

148. The vast majority of process philosophers follow Whitehead and Hartshorne in holding that divine power is purely persuasive. See, for example, Lewis S. Ford, "Divine Persuasion and the Triumph of Good," The Christian Scholar (1967), 135-150; and John B. Cobb, God and the World (Philadelphia: Westminster, 1969), 87-102. Others, however, like Williams and Pittenger, as I have indicated, have argued that some coerciveness is, in fact, exercised by the process God. My own feeling is that Hartshorne's process God acts persuasively (except in imposing the natural laws), but that the explicit justification of this position has not yet been forthcoming. See my "Process

Theism: Does a Persuasive God Coerce?," The Southern
Journal of Philosophy (1979), 133-143.   Nancy Frankenberry
more recently has argued that "between 'persuasion' and
'coercion' would seem to be a whole range of other modes of
power" unexploited by process thinkers: see her "Some
Problems in Process Theodicy," Religious Studies (1982),
179-197. Peter Hare and Edward Madden have protested that
process theology has given no good reasons "why God's power
should and must be exclusively persuasive," and insist that
"a certain amount of coercive power is morally required:"
see their "Evil and Persuasive Power," Process Studies
(1972), 44-48. See also three competent responses to Hare
and Madden: J. E. Barnhart's "Persuasive and Coercive
Power in Process Metaphysics," Process Studies (1973),
153-157; D. D. Baldwin's "Evil and Persuasive Power: A
Response to Hare and Madden," Process Studies (1973),
259-272; and David Griffin's God, Power, and Evil,
326-327. An equally competent and important study of the
issue is found in J. Gerald Janzen's "Modes of Power and
the Divine Relativity," Encounter (1975), 379-406.   Janzen
argues that the effort to conceive of God's activity solely
in terms of persuasion is misconceived and that "with
appropriate modifications, the two modes of divine power
[persuasion and coercion] can be fused into one model which
articulates that power in terms both of efficacy and of
finality, of coercion and persuasion" (405).

     149. D.   D.   Williams,   "Deity,   Monarchy,   and
Metaphysics: Whitehead's Critique of the Theological
Tradition," in I. Leclerc, ed., The Relevance of Whitehead
(New York: Humanities Press, 1961), 370.   See also his
"Time, Progress, and the Kingdom of God," in Brown, et.
al., Process Philosophy and Christian Thought (Indianapolis
and New York: Bobbs-Merrill, 1971), 441-463.   Williams
argues:
     Certainly it is true that God does exercise
     coercive power. We cannot escape that fact when
     we look at the way in which the structures of
     life coerce us, smash our plans, seize us in the
     grip of their inevitabilities.   God is not
     identical with those structures but His wrath is
     in them as they are related to the ultimate
     structure of value which is His own being.   But
     God also works persuasively; and His supreme
     resource is not coercive force, but the compel-
     ling power of His revelation in the Suffering
     Servant of all (461).

     150. Williams, "Deity, Monarchy, and Metaphysics,"
370-371.

151. Williams, "How Does God Act? An Essay in Whitehead's Metaphysics," in W. L. Reese and E. Freeman, eds., Process and Divinity (La Salle: Open Court, 1964), 177.

152. Pittenger, "Process Theology," The Expository Times (1973), 57.

153. Hartshorne, Man's Vision of God, 265.

154. Hartshorne, Man's Vision of God, 173.

155. Hartshorne, Man's Vision of God, 173. For a discussion of the applications of Hartshorne's thought to the question of pacifism and non-violence, see Barry L. Whitney, "Charles Hartshorne," in J. T. Culliton, ed., Non-Violence--Central to Christian Spirituality (New York and Toronto: The Edwin Mellen Press, 1982), 217-237. I argue that while non-violence is the ideal to be sought (implied by the persuasive God of process thought), pragmatic considerations render an absolute non-violence both dangerous and inappropriate.

156. Hartshorne, Whitehead's Philosophy, 164.

157. To be sure, the possibilities are not necessarily always pleasant. Lying in a hospital bed, for example, with death virtually imminent affords the rather limited possibilities of dying badly or dying well. God would lure us to the better of these so that we could attain the most value that was possible in an otherwise rather bleak situation.

158. Ford, "Whitehead's Differences from Hartshorne," 77.

159. Charles Hartshorne, "Santayana's Doctrine of Essence," in Paul A. Schilpp, ed., The Philosophy of George Santayana (Evanston and Chicago: Northwestern University Press, 1940), 151. Yet, see also Lewis Ford's critique of certain aspects of Hartshorne's position in his "Whitehead's Differences from Hartshorne," 58-83.

160. See Chapter 8, note 15. See also Barry L. Whitney, "Does God Influence the World's Creativity?: Hartshorne's Doctrine of Possibility," Philosophy Research Archives (1981), 613-622.

161. See note 127. See also Chapter 9 for a discussion of Hartshorne's aesthetic theory. I am grateful to Lewis Ford for his correspondence in response to my article on this issue (see note 160). He points out, I think validly, that the possibilities offered to a nascent occasion are limited to those which are actualizable in terms of the conditions of its past actual world, but that

the range of alternatives is itself <u>infinite</u>. Any dense continuum of possibilities, no matter how limited, has an infinity of alternatives (1983). The issue, nevertheless, is extremely complex. See Ford's essay in <u>Two Process Philosophers</u>.

162. See note 124, and Ford, "Whitehead's Differences from Hartshorne," 75-79.

163. This is the view not only of Hare and Madden, but of Daniel Day Williams. See notes 149-151 for references to Williams' writings; and Peter Hare and Edward Madden, <u>Evil and the Concept of God</u> (Springfield: C. C. Thomas, 1968), 121-122. See also their "Evil and Persuasive Power," 47. Yet in insisting, as Hare and Madden do, that without exercising some coercive intervention, God cannot guarantee the ultimate triumph of good, they demand a God who is, ultimately, all-controlling. See note 166 below.

164. Hick suggests the situation may be analogous to the relationship between a psychiatrist and a patient. The psychiatrist persuasively influences the patient to overcome his or her problems and to become "more free, to be and do what the patient really wants to be and do." God, in terms of this analogy, acts like the psychiatrist so as to persuade his creatures to act for good ends (Hick, "An Irenaean Theodicy," in Davis, ed., <u>Encountering Evil</u>,67). See also Hick, <u>Evil and the God of Love</u>, 344-345.

165. See note 132.

166. Against those critics who contend that without the power to intervene coercively the process God offers the world little hope that evils will be overcome or that a final good end will be guaranteed, Griffin has responded by pointing out that, among other things, any such divine interventions (or hope for such) would surely cause complacency among us. "There will be more basis for hope," he insists, "when people perceive that God's <u>modus operandi</u> is to save us <u>through</u> our activities, not in spite of them" ("Creation Out of Chaos and the Problem of Evil," in Davis, ed., <u>Encountering Evil</u>, 132). One must wonder, moreover, why a God who has the power to intervene coercively to overcome evil (as the God of classical theism is portrayed) has not in fact prevented the terrible agonies of the past. The reason may well be that God simply does <u>not</u> coercively intervene! Violating his own laws of nature and creaturely autonomy would be arbitrary acts to say the least, with no place to stop until the world was rid of all evil. But of course this would involve effectively ridding the world of all possibility for good. If we add to this the argument developed by Griffin that

God <u>cannot</u> intervene, even if he wanted to, the process position is even more clearly seen. Creatures, as such, necessarily have some independence, some autonomy. And indeed, without such creatures (were this even possible) God would be reduced to a mere monopolar abstraction.

PART THREE: PROCESS THEODICY

CHAPTER 8: EVIL AND FREE WILL

1. See Charles Hartshorne, "Panpsychism," in V. Ferm, ed., A History of Philosophical Systems (New York: Philosophical Library, 1950), 442-453.

2. Charles Hartshorne, Whitehead's Philosophy: Selected Essays, 1935-1970 (Lincoln: University of Nebraska Press, 1972), 44. See also Charles Hartshorne, Beyond Humanism: Essays in the New Philosophy of Nature (Chicago: Willett, Clark, 1937; reissued, Lincoln: University of Nebraska Press, 1968), 165.

3. Cited here is Reck's statement of Hartshorne's position. See Andrew J. Reck, The New American Philosophers (Baton Rouge: Louisiana State University Press, 1968). See also Charles Hartshorne, The Logic of Perfection and Other Essays in Neoclassical Metaphysics (La Salle: Open Court, 1962), 191; and Charles Hartshorne, The Philosophy and Psychology of Sensation (Chicago: University of Chicago Press, 1934; reissued, Port Washington: Kennikat Press, 1968), 11.

4. See Charles Hartshorne, Creative Synthesis and Philosophic Method (La Salle: Open Court, 1970), 48.

5. Hartshorne, Logic of Perfection, 217.

6. See Hartshorne, Logic of Perfection, 224-225.

7. The mental characteristics (at least in the higher forms of life) include emotions, memories, perceptions, and desires; the physical characteristics include size, shape, motion, vibration rate, etc. See Hartshorne, Logic of Perfection, 225.

8. Hartshorne, Logic of Perfection, 162-163.

9. Or, alternatively, "relative indeterminism." See Hartshorne, Creative Synthesis, 165.

10. See Hartshorne, Logic of Perfection, 162-163.

11. Charles Hartshorne, "Creativity and the Deductive Logic of Causality," Review of Metaphysics (1973), 65.

12. Charles Hartshorne, "Contingency and the New Era in Metaphysics," Journal of Philosophy (1932), 458. See also Charles Hartshorne, "Causal Necessities: An Alternative to Hume," Philosophical Review (1953), 479-499. Hartshorne also employs rather intricate reasonings in arguing that determinism is absolutely unverifiable, yet falsifiable both by human and divine experience. That reality as a "creative synthesis," however, is an a priori necessity which is verified by every experience and falsified by none. See Hartshorne, Creative Synthesis, 165-166.

13. Hartshorne, Creative Synthesis, 1.

14. Hartshorne, "Causal Necessities," 488.

15. Charles Hartshorne, Reality as Social Process: Studies in Metaphysics and Religion (Glencoe: The Free Press and Boston: The Beacon Press, 1953; reprinted by Hafner, 1971), 88-89. Hartshorne refers to the "infinity" of possibilities in a number of his writings: "between any given finite value which observation might fix as the probable maximum of the hypothetical irregularity, and the zero value which causality taken as absolute requires, there are an infinity of possible values, none of which is known to be more probable than another" ("Contingency and the New Era in Metaphysics," 426); "there is an eternal creative source of qualities such that, given any two actualized qualities, there is an inexhaustible possibility of intermediaries between them" ("Continuity, the Form of Forms, in Charles Peirce," Monist [1929], 527); "in addition to the aspects of the objects actually given there is an infinity of others virtually or potentially given" ("Husserl and the Social Structure of Immediacy," in M. Farber, ed., Philosophical Essays in Memory of Edmund Husserl [Cambridge: Harvard University Press, 1940], 220).

16. God sets the general limits for each cosmic epoch, while the more specific limits to the freedom of individual creatures, at each moment of their creative advance, are determined both by the creatures' immediate world (that is, the causal data) and by the decisions already made by the creatures in their sequence of experiences. See Chapter 7.

17. Charles Hartshorne, Man's Vision of God and the Logic of Theism (Chicago: Willett, Clark, 1941; reprinted

by Archon Books, Hamden, Conn., 1964), 30.

18. Hartshorne, Man's Vision of God, 30.

19. Charles Hartshorne, A Natural Theology for Our Time (La Salle: Open Court, 1967), 81.

20. Charles Hartshorne, "A New Look at the Problem of Evil," in F. C. Dommeyer, ed., Current Philosophical Issues: Essays in Honor of Curt John Ducasse (Springfield: C. C. Thomas, 1966), 208.

21. I think it is fair to assume that more and more theologians are moving away from the traditional doctrines of heaven and hell, conceived as literal places where one "goes" after death for rewards or punishment. Such a view is, as Berdyaev and others have pointed out, "the most disgusting morality ever conceived." See below, note 143.

22. H. J. McCloskey, "God and Evil," in N. Pike, ed., God and Evil (Englewood Cliffs: Prentice-Hall, 1964), 78 (originally published in The Journal of Bible and Religion [1962], 187-197).

23. For an excellent study of the various interpretations of miracles, see Ernst and Marie-Luise Keller, Miracles in Dispute (Philadelphia: Fortress Press, 1969).

24. See, for example, Rudolf Bultmann's existential, demythological interpretations of the New Testament's miracles. A valuable summary of Bultmann's interpretation of the miracles in the Gospel of John is given in Keller, Miracles in Dispute, 131-144.

25. This area is fast becoming one of the most exciting and important of interdisciplinary discussions. One recent symposium on "The Role of Belief in the Healing Process" (McMaster University, 1983), involved the active participation of philosophers, theologians, physicians, psychiatrists and anthropologists. See also the following: Raymond E. Brown, "The Gospel Miracles," in John L. McKenzie, ed., The Bible in Current Catholic Thought (New York: Herder and Herder, 1962), 184-201; Victor E. Frankl, The Doctor and the Soul: From Psychotherapy to Logotherapy (New York: Alfred A. Knopf, 1965); Claude A. Frazier, compiler, Faith Healing: Finger of God? Or Scientific Curiosity? (New York: Thomas Newson, 1973); Claude A. Frazier, ed., Healing and Religious Faith (Philadelphia: United Church Press, Pilgrim Press, 1974); R. H. Fuller, Interpreting the Miracles (London: SCM Press, 1971); Morton T. Kelsey, Healing and Christianity: In Ancient Thought and Modern Times (New York: Harper and Row, 1973); Francis MacNutt, Healing (Notre Dame: Ave Maria Press, 1974); Louis Monden,

Signs and Wonders; A Study of the Miraculous Element in Religion (New York: Desclee Co., 1966); Louis Rose, Faith Healing, Brian Morgan, ed. (Penguin Books, 1971); William W. Sargant, The Mind Possessed: A Physiology of Possession, Mysticism, and Faith Healing (Philadelphia: J. B. Lippincott, 1974); etc.

26. See P. A. Schilling, God and Human Anguish (Nashville: Abingdon, 1977), 174-181. Schilling argues, among other things, that even an "occasional suspension of the laws of gravitation [for example] because someone might fall off a rooftop or a cliff, would disrupt all forms of movement on sea or in the air, and render organized social life impossible" (175). Equally impossible would be the evolutionary development out of which life has evolved, to say nothing of intellectual pursuits and moral values.

27. Hartshorne, Creative Synthesis, 237.

28. Hartshorne, Creative Synthesis, 237-238.

29. Hartshorne, Creative Synthesis, 238.

30. Hartshorne, Creative Synthesis, 238.

31. Hartshorne, Creative Synthesis, 237.

32. Hartshorne, Reality as Social Process, 107.

33. See Ian Barbour's study of this point in his Issues in Science and Religion (New York: Harper and Row, 1966), 273-316.

34. Hartshorne, Reality as Social Process, 97.

35. Hartshorne, Logic of Perfection, 169.

36. See, Schilling, God and Human Anguish, 176-177.

37. J. L. Mackie, "Evil and Omnipotence," in Pike, ed., God and Evil, 56 (originally published in Mind [1955], 200-212). See also Antony Flew, "Divine Omnipotence and Human Freedom," in A. Flew and Alasdair MacIntyre, eds., New Essays in Philosophical Theology (London: SCM, 1955), 144-169.

38. Mackie, "Evil and Omnipotence," 56-57.

39. I should think that a strict, literalistic interpretation of the Bible is no longer held by increasing numbers of theologians. The creation accounts, accordingly, and other passages (for example, Adam and Eve's "fall" from paradise) are now seen existentially or symbolically. See William J. Duggan, Myth and Christian Belief (Notre Dame: Fides Publishers, 1971).

40. On this point John Hick argues that the literal reading of the Genesis "fall" of man, as it is presented in the Augustinian tradition, "presents the wanton paradox of

man (or the angels) being placed as finitely perfect
creatures in a finitely perfect environment and then
becoming the locus of the self-creation of evil ex
nihilo." Yet, as Hick points out, "[t]o say that an
unqualifiedly good (though finite) being gratuitously sins
is to say that he was not unqualifiedly good in the first
place:" see John Hick, Evil and the God of Love (New
York: Harper and Row, 1966; revised 1978), 174.

41. See Part Two, note 88.

42. Hartshorne, Creative Synthesis, 238. I have
taken this phrase somewhat out of context. In its proper
context, Hartshorne is explaining why only God can act
wholly with goodness. Creatures feel pressured to act in
their own interests. "But to be infinitely good is...a
divine attribute. To suppose that it could be a human one
by a law of nature or divine decree seems to amount to
supposing that the ideal form of the voluntary could be
entirely involuntary. Only God needs no choice to be
good--he alone is goodness in its ideal form."

43. McCloskey, "God and Evil," 80.

44. Peter H. Hare and Edward H. Madden, Evil and the
Concept of God (Springfield: C.C. Thomas, 1968), 74.

45. Hare and Madden, Evil and the Concept of God, 74.

46. Hartshorne, Creative Synthesis, 239.

47. See Ninian Smart, "Omnipotence, Evil and
Supermen," in Pike, ed., God and Evil, 103-112 (originally
published in Philosophy [1961], 188-195).

48. Smart, "Omnipotence, Evil and Supermen," 106.

49. In the second century, Irenaeus made this point,
without the benefit of modern scientific evolutionary
theory. See Hick's discussion in his Evil and the God of
Love, 211-215.

50. An exception, however, is Teilhard de Chardin,
whose version of process thought differs from the
Whiteheadian-Hartshornean version in that (among other
things) he sees the process ending in a final and complete
perfection. See Ian Barbour, "Teilhard's Process
Metaphysics," The Journal of Religion (1969), 136-159.

51. Yet, see David Griffin's critique of Hick's
theodicy in his God, Power and Evil: A Process Theodicy
(Philadelphia: Westminster, 1976), 174-204. See also
Griffin's critique and Hick's response in Stephen T. Davis,
ed., Encountering Evil (Atlanta: John Knox Press,
1981), 53-55 and 63-68.

52. See McCloskey, "God and Evil," 77, emphasis removed.

53. See McCloskey," God and Evil," 77.

CHAPTER 9: AESTHETIC VALUE AND THE OVERCOMING OF EVIL

54. Hartshorne, Creative Synthesis, 306.

55. Hartshorne, Creative Synthesis, 304.

56. Charles Hartshorne, Born to Sing: An Interpretation and World Survey of Bird Song (Bloomington: Indiana University Press, 1973), 8.

57. Hartshorne, Creative Synthesis, 307; Born to Sing, 8.

58. See Hartshorne, Creative Synthesis, 306.

59. Hartshorne, Creative Synthesis, 304.

60. Hartshorne, Born to Sing, 6.

61. See Hartshorne, Born to Sing, 6-7.

62. This example was given by Hartshorne in a paper titled, "The Ultimacy of Aesthetic Principles," delivered at a conference on aesthetics, in Vancouver, Canada (1980), 13.

63. See Hartshorne, "The Ultimacy of Aesthetic Principles," 13.

64. Hartshorne, Creative Synthesis, 304.

65. Hartshorne, Man's Vision of God, 216.

66. See especially his Born to Sing, passim.

67. Hartshorne, Creative Synthesis, 307.

68. Hartshorne, Creative Synthesis, 307.

69. Hartshorne, Creative Synthesis, 308-309; see also, Born to Sing, 8.

70. John Cobb and David Griffin, Process Theology (Philadelphia: Westminster, 1976), 73.

71. Alfred North Whitehead, Process and Reality (New York: Macmillan, 1929), 169. See Griffin, God, Power, and Evil, 286.

72. Whitehead, Process and Reality, 161. See Griffin, God, Power, and Evil, 287.

73. Whitehead, Process and Reality, 381. See Griffin, God, Power, and Evil, 287.

74. See Hartshorne, "The Ultimacy of Aesthetic Principles," 18; see also Chapter 8.

75. See Hartshorne, Creative Synthesis, 311-312.

76. Hartshorne, Creative Synthesis, 311.

77. Hartshorne, Creative Synthesis, 311.

78. Hartshorne, Creative Synthesis, 312.

79. Griffin, God, Power, and Evil, 294.

80. Schilling, God and Human Anguish, 179.

81. Griffin, God, Power, and Evil, 308.

82. See Griffin, God, Power, and Evil, 308.

83. Griffin, God, Power, and Evil, 309. Should God, asks Griffin, for the sake of avoiding the possibility of people like Hitler, have precluded the possibility of others like Jesus, Leonardo da Vinci, the Buddha, and millions of other marvellous, loving, and creative human beings? In a critique of Griffin's theodicy, Stephen Davis has argued that "the world is not worthwhile as it stands," and that without redemption by God and, more precisely, without the guarantee that the risk of evil involved in creating the world was worth taking, it would indeed have been better that human beings had never been created. Yet Griffin's response is surely valid: it would be presumptuous for anyone to assume that, while his own life may be worthwhile, the lives of others are not intrinsically valuable (see Davis, ed., Encountering Evil, 128 and 135). And indeed, as Hartshorne has argued so eloquently, life as such is aesthetically valuable, to some degree at least. I would add that even if the world were in fact to collapse into a terrible, terminal anguish and chaos, the fact that we were free and autonomous creatures was worth this fatal risk. The values attained by free creatures would not be cancelled out by the destruction of the world. See Chapters 8 and 9.

84. Griffin, God, Power, and Evil, 309.

85. Griffin, God, Power, and Evil, 310. There are, however, critics who argue that process thought unjustifiably places aesthetic concerns over ethical ones. Hare and Madden, for example, contend that "a God who is willing to pay any amount in moral and physical evil to

gain aesthetic value is an unlovable being" (Peter Hare and Edward Madden, "Evil and Unlimited Power," Review of Metaphysics [1966], 287). The process God, they contend, "sacrifices human feelings to aesthetic ends" (Hare and Madden, Evil and the Concept of God, 124). Likewise, Stephen Ely argues that since for process thought "[a]ll values are . . . fundamentally aesthetic . . . . God . . . is not concerned with any finite sufferings, difficulties, and triumphs--except as material for his aesthetic delight. God, we must say definitely, is not primarily good. He does not will the good. He wills the beautiful." "God's feelings alone are considered of importance," and "the actualities of the world can at best be but instruments of God's joy," merely "fragments of a pattern that they cannot ever appreciate" (S. Ely, The Religious Availability of Whitehead's God [Madison: University of Wisconsin Press, 1942], 52, 48). More recently, John Hick has criticized process thought on the same grounds: the process God, he contends, is the God of the "elite," the God of "the great and successful among mankind," but not the God of the countless millions who suffer in wasted lives (John Hick, Philosophy of Religion [Englewood Cliffs: Prentice-Hall, 1983], third edition, 55). Hick's point is that the aesthetic criterion of value in process thought wrongly justifies all the evil and misery in the world as necessary by-products of the great goods which have evolved: "the good that has occurred renders worthwhile all the wickedness that has been committed and all the suffering that has been endured"(55).

It is difficult to respond to these critiques in brief, for quite a few issues are involved. Some of these have already been discussed in the text, of course, but a few additional points can be made. I would refer the reader, first of all, to Griffin's response both to Hare and Madden and to Ely. Griffin points out that the arguments of these critics are largely invalidated, since, among other things, they have misinterpreted what Whitehead means by "beauty" and "aesthetic" enjoyment (see Griffin, God, Power, and Evil, 301-302). Hartshorne, furthermore, has likewise responded both to Ely and to Hare and Madden, respectively, in his Whitehead's Philosophy, 102-110, and his "The Dipolar Conception of Deity," Review of Metaphysics (1967), 282-289. Hartshorne underscores the fundamental point that process can proceed only with great goods and great evils being produced. The goods are not possible without the risk of evils, and if the process were to eliminate such evils, it could do so only at the cost of goods; yet this would be itself an evil, the evil of unnecessary triviality, and the lapse into such "negligible value" would cause "the destruction of all values whatever"

(Hartshorne, Whitehead's Philosophy, 104). Hartshorne
insists, further, that despite Spinoza and Leibniz, no one
has shown "the conceivability of an exhaustive or a best
actualization of possible good." It "is the critic's
fantasy" that somehow great good can exist without evil
(Hartshorne, "The Dipolar Conception," 286).

He argues, further, that all life is, as such, a good,
for every experience has aesthetic value. The critics, on
the other hand, seem to believe the opposite, that life is
basically evil, since (according to Hick, for example)
"[f]or each . . .'marvellous human being,' perhaps tens of
thousands of others have existed without any significant
degree of personal freedom and without any opportunity for
intellectual, moral, aesthetic, or spiritual development,
their lives spent in a desperate and degrading struggle to
survive" (Hick, Philosophy of Religion, 54). Hartshorne,
of course, does not deny the existence of such suffering
and misery, but the point remains that God could have
prevented this only by not having lured the primordial
chaos into a world order. There is no validity in saying
that the God of process thought is satisfied that such evil
exists and that it is all justifiable because of the good
which also exists: God seeks ever greater opportunities
for good, for significant aesthetic achievement; he does
not seek suffering and evil nor does he smugly condone them.

Hartshorne has responded also to the critics'
"suspicion of divine egoism in the fact that Whitehead says
beauty is more fundamental than truth and that even
goodness is the aim at beauty" (Hartshorne, Whitehead's
Philosophy, 107). The triumvirate, "goodness, truth and
... beauty," that is, "acting rightly, thinking rightly,
and experiencing well or satisfyingly," ought to be
reversed: beauty is the "basic value," and in it both
goodness and truth are supposed (see Hartshorne, Creative
Synthesis, 303). Truth is a form of aesthetic value "since
the more truth one knows, the more one can order and also
diversify one's ideas and make them fit one's
perceptions . . . . It is more illuminating to take truth
as a form of beauty than beauty as a form of truth."
Likewise, goodness "presupposes aesthetics," since goodness
"is not the value of experiences themselves, but rather the
instrumental value of acting so as to increase the
intrinsic value of future experiences, particularly those
of others than oneself" (Hartshorne, Creative Synthesis,
308). Hartshorne points out that what Whitehead and he
mean by beauty (aesthetic value) is, simply, "happiness."
"God seeks the happiness of each creature as elements in
his own happiness. Clearly this is not aestheticism in any
sense in which there is conflict with ethical

considerations. The ethical side comes in through the social character of being, which makes the aim at beauty not just for self, and also makes it include, as a supreme form of beauty, the beauty of companionship and generosity" (Hartshorne, Whitehead's Philosophy, 107-108). Since "goodness is the disinterested will to enhance the value of future experiences, ethics presupposes aesthetics" (Hartshorne, Creative Synthesis, 308). The primacy of aesthetics is established, furthermore, by the observation that whereas animals do not experience ethical goods and evils, they do experience aesthetic value. Likewise, ethical values are not applicable to God: God's goodness is ever constant, while he continually grows aesthetically (see Hartshorne, Creative Synthesis, 308-310).

86. Charles Hartshorne, "Immortality of the Past: Critique of a Prevalent Misinterpretation," Review of Metaphysics (1953), 106.

87. Hartshorne, "Immortality of the Past," 106.

88. Hartshorne, "Immortality of the Past," 110.

89. Hartshorne, The Divine Relativity: A Social Conception of God (New Haven: Yale University Press, 1948), 46.

90. Hartshorne, "Immortality of the Past," 102.

91. Hartshorne, "Immortality of the Past," 107.

92. Hartshorne, "Immortality of the Past," 102. See also Divine Relativity, 46.

93. Many thinkers focus on the problem of gratuitous evil as the main issue which confronts the theist. They grant that the existence of an all-powerful and all-good God may be reconcilable with some evil, but surely, they contend, much of the world's evil seems purely gratuitous. (See, for example, the recent study by Michael Peterson, Evil and the Christian God [Grand Rapids, MI: Baker Book House], 1982). From the perspective of process theodicy, however, the issue of accounting for apparently useless and meaningless evil is readily answered: Hartshorne contends that there simply is no "utterly senseless" or "unredeemed evil." "Any evil has some value from some perspective, for even to know it exists is to make it contributory to a good, knowledge itself being a good" (Natural Theology, 80, emphasis added). Even the devastating cancer cells, for example, achieve a degree of aesthetic value appropriate to their needs (see Hartshorne, "A New Look at the Problem of Evil," 205). This is not to say, however, that Hartshorne believes that all evils are really parts of a good whole or means to a good end. Nor does he believe that the world is a perfect whole, ordained as such by God. Hartshorne's point, rather, is that it is not the task of theodicy to

try to justify individual evils as such. The reason for evils in general can be explained as a result of the creativity of the world's creatures, but particular evils "have no ultimate reason" and are simply "nonrational." "Risk of evil and opportunity for good are two aspects of just one thing, multiple freedom" (Natural Theology, 81), and there is no guarantee that individual creatures (including those on the microscopic level) will not produce evils with little redeeming value for others. And yet, every experience --every good and every evil--has "some value from some perspective."

94. Hartshorne, Divine Relativity, 46.

95. Hartshorne, Whitehead's Philosophy, 106.

96. Ely, Religious Availability of Whitehead's God, 48.

97. Ely, Religious Availability of Whitehead's God, 41.

98. Hartshorne, Whitehead's Philosophy, 103.

99. Hartshorne, Whitehead's Philosophy, 103.

100. Hartshorne, Whitehead's Philosophy, 104.

101. Whitehead, Process and Reality, 532. See Hartshorne, "Immortality of the Past," 111.

102. Griffin, God, Power, and Evil, 303.

103. Whitehead, Process and Reality, 532. See Griffin, God, Power, and Evil, 305.

104. See Griffin, God, Power, and Evil, 305-308.

105. Hartshorne, Man's Vision of God, 172.

106. Whitehead, Process and Reality, 54.

107. Hartshorne, Man's Vision of God, 331.

108. Whitehead, Process and Reality, 532.

109. Hartshorne, Creative Synthesis, 241.

110. Hartshorne, Creative Synthesis, 241.

111. Hartshorne, "Immortality of the Past," 111.

112. See Hartshorne, Creative Synthesis, 241.

113. Hartshorne, "Immortality of the Past," 101. Hartshorne acknowledges that "such terms as 'impulse' will appear crude and degrading in application to God, but the point is that any psychological term, such as 'will' or 'knowledge,' is equally so, unless taken analogically rather than literally."

114. There are, however, several process thinkers who have made a case for subjective immortality within a Whiteheadian framework: see note 170.

115. Hick, Evil and the God of Love, 338.

116. Hick, Evil and the God of Love, 340.

117. See, Charles Hartshorne, "Philosophy After Fifty Years," in Peter A. Bertocci, ed., Mid-Twentieth Century American Philosophy: Personal Statements (New York: Humanities Press, 1974), 147.

118. Hartshorne, Reality as Social Process, 211.

119. Hartshorne, Whitehead's Philosophy, 134. (Hartshorne here is citing Whitehead).

120. Charles Hartshorne, Theology in Crisis: A Colloquium on The Credibility of "God" (New Concord: Muskingum College, 1967), 49. Hartshorne has two essays in this book: "God and the Social Structure of Reality" and "The Significance of Man in the Life of God." Schubert Ogden's essay, "Toward a New Theism," is also included, as are several pages of questions, with responses by Hartshorne and Ogden.

121. See Hartshorne, Logic of Perfection, 251-252.

122. Hartshorne, Logic of Perfection, 252.

123. Hartshorne, Logic of Perfection, 253.

124. Hartshorne, Reality as Social Process, 211.

125. See Charles Hartshorne, "A Philosopher's Assessment of Christianity," in Walter Leibrecht, ed., Religion and Culture: Essays in Honor of Paul Tillich (New York: Harper, 1959), 177-178. See also Hartshorne, Whitehead's Philosophy, 108-109.

126. Hartshorne, Logic of Perfection, 254.

127. Hartshorne, Logic of Perfection, 253.

128. Hartshorne, Logic of Perfection, 253.

129. See Hartshorne, Theology in Crisis, 40.

130. See Hartshorne, "Philosophy After Fifty Years," 149.

131. See Hartshorne, Whitehead's Philosophy, 105-106.

132. Hartshorne, Whitehead's Philosophy, 106.

133. See Charles Hartshorne, "Religion in Process Philosophy," in J. Clayton Feaver and William Horosz, eds., Religion in Philosophical and Cultural Perspective (Princeton: D. Van Nostrand, 1967), 264.

134. Hartshorne, "Religion in Process Philosophy," 265.

135. Hartshorne, "Religion in Process Philosophy," 265.

136. Hartshorne, Logic of Perfection, 259-260.

137. Hartshorne, "Philosophy After Fifty Years," 145.

138. See Hartshorne, "Philosophy After Fifty Years," 145; see also Hartshorne, "Religion in Process Philosophy," 266-267.

139. Hartshorne, "A Philosopher's Assessment of Christianity," 176.

140. Hartshorne, "A Philosopher's Assessment of Christianity," 176.

141. Hartshorne, "A Philosopher's Assessment of Christianity," 176.

142. See Hartshorne, "Philosophy After Fifty Years," 147.

143. Hartshorne, "Religion in Process Philosophy," 264.

144. Hartshorne, Logic of Perfection, 255.

145. Hartshorne, Logic of Perfection, 255.

146. Hartshorne, "A Philosopher's Assessment of Christianity," 177.

147. Hartshorne, Logic of Perfection, 257.

148. See Hartshorne, Theology in Crisis, 43.

149. Hartshorne, Theology in Crisis, 42.

150. Hartshorne, Theology in Crisis, 43.

151. See Hartshorne, Logic of Perfection, 259-262.

152. Hartshorne, Logic of Perfection, 259.

153. Hartshorne, Logic of Perfection, 260.

154. Hartshorne, Logic of Perfection, 261.

155. Hartshorne, Logic of Perfection, 261.

156. See Hartshorne, Logic of Perfection, 261-262.

157. Hartshorne, Logic of Perfection, 261.

158. See Hartshorne, "Philosophy After Fifty Years," 150.

159. Hartshorne, "Philosophy After Fifty Years," 151.

160. Hartshorne, "Philosophy After Fifty Years," 150.

161. Hartshorne, Logic of Perfection, 262.

162. Hartshorne, Logic of Perfection, 262.

163. Hartshorne, Whitehead's Philosophy, 106-107.

164. Hartshorne, Whitehead's Philosophy, 107.

165. Hartshorne, Whitehead's Philosophy, 107. (Hartshorne here is citing Whitehead).

166. Hartshorne, "Philosophy After Fifty Years," 149.

167. See Hartshorne, "Philosophy After Fifty Years," 149; see also Hartshorne, Logic of Perfection, 251.

168. Hartshorne, "Philosophy After Fifty Years," 149.

169. Hartshorne, "A Philosopher's Assessment of Christianity," 177.

170. Hartshorne, Reality as Social Process, 211. There are, to be sure, several process thinkers who have argued that Whitehead's system can accommodate subjective immortality. See, for example, David Griffin, "The Possibility of Subjective Immortality in Whitehead's Philosophy," Modern Schoolman (1975), 39-57; Lewis S. Ford and Marjorie Suchocki, "A Whiteheadian Reflection on Subjective Immortality," Process Studies (1977), 1-13; and Marjorie Suchochi, "The Question of Immortality," Journal of Religion (1977), 288-306. These arguments are impressive, and show clearly that Whiteheadian process thought does not exclude subjective immortality. My point, nevertheless, is that the possibility of subjective immortality is not necessary to ensure the value and meaning of our lives. Neither is it an indispensable ingredient in a viable theodicy: value and meaning are accounted for by objective immortality, and without the problems which attend subjective immortality (for example, the question of a meaningful personal identity throughout infinite time, and the necessity of any afterlife containing both goods and evils, and so on, as discussed in this chapter).

CHAPTER 10:   CONCLUSION

171. See, for example, Nancy Frankenberry, "Some Problems in Process Theodicy," Religious Studies (1982), 193-195. "What," she asks, "can possibly be a religious

meaning of redemption in an evolutionary universe of great
unpredictability, risk, chance, loss, and unimaginable
emergent potentiality?" (193). And since process thought
offers no future world of eternal existence for human
beings, she finds its theodicy problematic. I can share
her hope for "subjective immortality," but I wonder if
Hartshorne's arguments against this possibility do not
express the more convincing position.

172. Hartshorne, "A New Look at the Problem of Evil,"
204.

173. Hartshorne, "A New Look at the Problem of Evil,"
204.

174. See Chapter 7 and Part II, note 124.

175. There is no question that Hartshorne's God
imposes the natural laws, but is this act done persuasively
or coercively? My point is not that it is, beyond any
doubt, coercive, but only that Hartshorne has not fully
justified its being persuasive. In a 1974 letter in
response to my questioning of this point, Hartshorne
suggested that in imposing the natural laws God in fact
"persuades all creatures to respond to certain patterns of
order....The response is only approximately and
statistically determined by the 'lure of the pattern'". As
such, it is "not absolutely but relatively irresistible."
He has written elsewhere on this point: "A divine
prehension can use its freedom to create, and for a
suitable period maintain, a particular world order. This
selection then becomes a persuasive 'lure', an irrestible
datum, for all ordinary acts of synthesis" (Whitehead's
Philosophy, 164). "God molds us, by presenting at each
moment a partly new ideal or order of preference which our
unself-conscious awareness takes as object, and thus
renders influential upon our entire activity" (Divine
Relativity, 142). Yet despite such statements, the issue
is far from clear, to me at least. I remain unconvinced
that the divine act of imposing natural laws is justifiably
termed persuasive. Despite Ford and Whitehead, I see no
objection, furthermore, to God imposing natural laws:
indeed, I see this as necessary. And neither do I have an
objection to these laws being coercively imposed, for they
do not infringe absolutely upon creaturely freedom. They
merely restrict it to certain limitations (and in fact make
freedom itself possible). It seems to me that without a
distinction between God's general limits (the natural laws
for a particular cosmic epoch) and more specific limits,
the latter defining what possibilities are realizable in
the far more limited circumstances of each individual
creature's life, this issue has become unnecessarily

confused. Both types of limits restrict creaturely freedom, but God alone imposes the general limits, while the creature's past world determines the specific limits within which that creature can operate. I would define the former as divine coercion, but not the latter. With respect to the latter, God acts persuasively in luring creatures toward the best possible ideals, given the limitations imposed by the past world of the creature.

176. See Ford, "Whitehead's Differences from Hartshorne," 75-79.

177. See J. Gerald Janzen, "Modes of Power and Divine Relativity," Encounter (1975), 379-406. Despite his lengthy and impressive argument that the process God exerts both persuasive and coercive power, I do not find Janzen's argument convincing. I think Ford's criticism is valid: Janzen's God mediates the past to present events, but this is hardly a coercive act since the past events themselves restrict the range of possibilities open to the present event. It is not further restricted (coercively) by God in his mediating activity. See L.S. Ford, The Lure of God (Philadelphia: Fortress Press, 1978), 43.

178. See Chapter 7 and the references in notes 149-151. See also his God's Grace and Man's Hope (New York: Harper and Brothers, 1949). For a brief discussion of Williams' view, see Warren McWilliams, "Daniel Day Williams' Vulnerable and Invulnerable God," Encounter (1983), 73-89.

179. Griffin has distinguished between "absolute coercion" and "relative coercion". The former refers to a complete determining of an event by another agent, a possibility rejected by process metaphysics. "Relative coercion," however, refers to coercive elements involved in what is essentially a persuasive efficient causation. Such coercion "is not antithetical to the fact that all individuals have some self-determining freedom so that all power upon them is ultimately persuasive." Griffin explains that the past data of an agent must be prehended by the agent, that the past determines what is received by the agent, and that the past determines how the new agent will initially respond to what it receives. Yet despite these "coercive" elements of limitation, the agent nevertheless is free to decide precisely how to respond to the data it receives from the past. Acknowledging that there are coercive limitations on every free agent is, as Griffin suggests, "simply another way of saying that there is no absolute freedom" (Griffin, God, Power, and Evil, 326).

180. There are other issues which are in need of further discussion. In particular, I would suggest that the question concerning divine creation <u>ex</u> <u>nihilo</u> versus creation out of previous materials requires much more attention. See Chapter 6 and Part Two, note 64. The question, furthermore, concerning subjective immortality perhaps ought to be looked at more closely. Is subjective immortality essential to Christianity and to a viable theodicy? I have supported Hartshorne's argument that it is not, yet I do not feel certain the last word on this issue has been said.

SUBJECT INDEX

NAME INDEX

TORONTO STUDIES IN THEOLOGY